SOUNDTRACK

SOUNDTRACK

A FORTY-DAY PLAYLIST THROUGH THE PSALMS

J. D. Walt

The psalm for each day's reflection is taken from
http://psalms.seedbed.com/psalter

Unless otherwise indicated, all other Scripture quotations are taken from
the Holy Bible, New International Version®, NIV®. Copyright © 1973,
1978, 1984, 2011 by Biblica, Inc.™ Used by permission of Zondervan.
All rights reserved worldwide. www.zondervan.com

Scripture quotations marked THE MESSAGE are from THE MESSAGE by
Eugene H. Peterson. © 1993, 1994, 1995, 1996, 2000. Used by permission
of NavPress Publishing Group. All rights reserved.

Scriptures marked NASB are from the NEW AMERICAN STANDARD
BIBLE®, © The Lockman Foundation 1960, 1962, 1963, 1968, 1971, 1972,
1973, 1975, 1977, 1995. Used by permission.

Scriptures marked NLT are from the Holy Bible, New Living Translation.
© 1996, 2004, 2007. Used by permission of Tyndale House Publishers,
Inc., Carol Stream, Illinois 60188. All rights reserved.

Scripture quotations marked ESV are from The Holy Bible, English
Standard Version®, ESV®, copyright © 2001 by Crossway Bibles, a division
of Good News Publishers. Used by permission. All rights reserved.

Scripture quotations marked DV are from the Douay-Rheims Bible.

Printed in the United States of America

Paperback ISBN: 978-1-62824-144-0
Mobi ISBN: 978-1-62824-145-7
ePub ISBN: 978-1-62824-172-3
uPDF ISBN: 978-1-62824-173-0

Library of Congress Control Number: 2015944097

*Cover illustration and cover design by Nikabrik Design
Page design by PerfecType, Nashville, TN*

SEEDBED PUBLISHING
Franklin, Tennessee
seedbed.com
SOW FOR A GREAT AWAKENING

CONTENTS

ACKNOWLEDGMENTS

This book is but the tip of the iceberg of a much larger project, which must be duly acknowledged before going one step further. Many have lamented the loss of psalm-singing in the modern church, but few have gone beyond their lament to do anything about it. Julie and Timothy Tennent took on the challenge. Together they embarked on the gargantuan challenge of translating all 150 psalms into the poetic, metrical format of a Psalter. Standing on the shoulders of the giants of this craft from across the centuries, they crafted psalm after psalm after psalm into the rhythms and rhymes that will freight this practice for a new century of psalm singers. The most beautiful part of the whole project, in my estimation, is the way they went about the work. It happened in the early light of a thousand mornings as they together sang their way through these ancient songs in worship to Almighty God. On behalf of many, I want to thank them for this liturgical labor of love.

Soundtrack: A Forty-Day Playlist through the Psalms is a small effort to shed light on this big aspiration of restoring psalm-singing to new generations of followers of Jesus in our time. I offer it as tribute to Timothy and Julie, my dear friends, mentors, and co-laborers in the global mission of the gospel.

Thanks are also in order to Kristin Gelinas, a close friend and colleague of the Tennents, who served consistently as a wise collaborative partner and constantly as a meticulous editorial assistant on the larger Psalter project on which this book is built. Holly Jones, our production director at Seedbed Publishing, skillfully shepherded the complex process of bringing the book you hold in your hands into being. Nick Perreault brought the vinyl-esque vibey design to the project. Finally, I want to thank my friend and colleague, Andy Miller, who has labored faithfully for decades to master the myriad disciplines of publishing and has shepherded the team, which has become the house that is Seedbed Publishing.

Sola sancta caritas!

John David Walt Jr.
The Day of Epiphany 2016

INTRODUCTION

Have you been to a wedding lately? They've changed. Yes, they still do vows and rings, bridesmaids and groomsmen, and at times, sappy made-up vows. The change comes at the reception. Sure, there's cake and punch and the usual toasts and niceties. And yes, there's the traditional first dance and so forth.

The big change comes in what happens next. Sometime over the past couple of decades someone had the idea to hire a deejay; that took the wedding reception to a whole new level. The song selections can consume quite a lot of attention. I've known couples that actually got into some pretty big fights over the playlists for these festive occasions.

Why is a playlist so important? These playlists serve as a kind of intergenerational soundtrack. Nothing has the power to unite different generations quite like a song. There's just nothing like that moment at a wedding reception when the deejay cues up the 1976 golden one-hit wonder "Play That Funky Music"! Everyone (from grandmas to toddlers) hits the floor with bodily contortions usually reserved for football games and shuffleboard tournaments. Somehow everyone knows the words and they sing it with an almost liturgical exuberance. The corporate singing of songs has a way of doing this like nothing else. If you don't believe me, just behold what happens when someone turns up the volume on the wonder song of 1978 by none other than Village People. You know it: "YMCA."

Now that you are with me, you may be pondering the point I'm trying to make. This notion of an intergenerational catalog of songs sung together by men, women, and children from every tongue, tribe, and nation across the earth was God's original idea. In fact, God has actually written these songs down in a book, and this book can be found in the very heart and center of the Book of all books, the Bible. See where this is going? Yes, I'm talking about the book of Psalms.

Something that came so naturally to generations of God's people before, now seems utterly foreign to us. Who sings the Psalms? Answer: monks, nuns, and the occasional Presbyterian church.

People of God! The Psalms are our soundtrack!

It's time we start singing them again. Why? That's what this little book is all about. Melody transforms a message into a movement. Said another way, it takes a "groove-ment" to start a movement. The Psalms groove our soul with the soundtrack of God.

Speaking of groove, vinyl is making a comeback in the music recording industry. Have you ever thought about how a vinyl record gets made? First, the sound waves of live music are recorded onto a tape reel. Next, these sound waves are transmitted through a sapphire stylus (think—very expensive writing instrument), which literally cuts a groove into the master record, etching the intricacies of the sound waves onto the record. Next, the now-grooved master record is pressed against a circular piece of vinyl, imprinting the grooves onto the vinyl record. To listen to the record, we place it on a turntable where another stylus (we called it a needle back in the day) reads the sound waves and transmits them through speakers, amplifying the sound. It's hard to imagine that we refer to such a complex, beautiful process like this as *analog*. So let me make the "analog-y" that you've already started to process.

The Psalms are the master record. We are the vinyl. God, our Father, by the inspiration of the Holy Spirit, engaged the lathe-like stylus of people like David and Asaph and other worship leaders of the day to cut deep, intricate grooves of melody and message into the lives of the people of God. This music was recorded onto scrolls and later pressed into books and now comes to us in the format we call the Psalms.

Henceforth, I'll not be calling them the Psalms. Rather, I will refer to the 150-track playlist at the center of our Bibles as the Songs. Yes, it is without rival the best-selling record of all times.

Now, speaking of analog, this is our challenge. If ever we could appropriately use the term *analog,* it would have to be with respect to the recording of the Songs. All we have are the words. It would be akin to someone giving you the liner notes of your favorite band's most recent record without the record. You would look at the person and perhaps use some version of this poignant phrase of my nine-year-old son, "What the what?!"

That's what we are dealing with. We've managed to content ourselves with the liner notes of the best-selling record of all times. What started out as the Spirit-inspired heart cries of the human race grooving the Word of God into the ruts of their lives now comes to us mostly in the polished tones of Elizabethan English.

We rave about those lyrics, as we should, but what if we could sing them again? The ancient melodies are lost forever; it's probably for the best because every generation must make its own melody.

It brings us to the idea of a metrical Psalter. Sure, there's good old Gregorian chant, but the Protestant Reformation brought a new form of psalm-singing into the church. A metrical Psalter is a type of Bible translation wherein the Psalms are formed into vernacular poetry that can be sung like a hymn in a particular meter (think metronome). In other words, the Psalms are translated into lyrically rhyming stanzas so they can be sung to a variety of commonly known hymn tunes.

Here's an example of how this works. Following are the words from Psalm 100 (NIV).

> Shout for joy to the LORD, all the earth.
> Worship the LORD with gladness;
> come before him with joyful songs.
> Know that the LORD is God.
> It is he who made us, and we are his;
> we are his people, the sheep of his pasture.
>
> Enter his gates with thanksgiving
> and his courts with praise;
> give thanks to him and praise his name.
> For the LORD is good and his love endures forever;
> his faithfulness continues through all generations.

The following is Psalm 100 arranged in common meter (86.86). This simply means there is a repeating pattern of eight syllables in one line and six syllables in the next line. One of the most well-known hymns in the world, "Amazing Grace," is written in common meter. Try singing Psalm 100 as written below to the tune of "Amazing Grace."

Shout joyfully unto the LORD;
Let all the earth now sing!
Come worship; serve with gladsome heart,
Your songs before Him bring.

Know that the LORD Himself is God,
He made us; not ourselves;
We are His people and His sheep;
His pasture's where we dwell.

Enter His gates with thanksgiving,
Into His courts with praise.
Give thanks to Him and bless His name,
Your praises sing always.

For God is good, His love endures,
Forever it does last;
His faithfulness from age to age,
Till life and time are past.

That's how you sing a metrical psalm, and that's how this little book will work. Each day will offer a psalm from our Seedbed Psalter followed by a short reflection authored by yours truly. I recommend reading the psalm through slowly first. Next read the reflection. Finally, try singing the psalm.

Why are we doing this? We are doing this because some words were meant to be sung and not just for singing's sake, but for the sake of our souls. This will be different, so give it time. Because we will be working with some pretty old hymn tunes, it's just not going to sound as cool as the latest song from Jesus Culture. Stick with it anyway. We will provide resources to help with the singing at **soundtrack.seedbed.com**.

Dietrich Bonhoeffer wrote, "Whenever the Psalter is abandoned, an incomparable treasure vanishes from the Christian church. With its recovery will come unsuspected power."[1]

When Scripture and song—two of the greatest realities in the universe—come together, unsuspected power starts flowing. It brings me to close where I began, with wedding parties. Do you realize at the heart of the heart of the heart of Scripture a song is playing? It is commonly referred to as the Song of Songs. The song, in its core essence, consists of five primal Hebrew words: *my, beloved, mine, I, his* (Song of Songs 2:16a).

That's it. In the deepest heart of the Word of God sings this song of all songs. It never stops playing. We might consider it as the groove of eternity. The Father sings this song over the church, the bride of his Son, in a melody only the Holy Spirit can sound. Yes, this song underwrites and underscores the entire soundtrack of the Psalms.

This song of songs will play without pause until one bright day when the sky will seem to roll back as a scroll. The doors of heaven will fling wide open and we, the bride of Christ, will behold the image of the One by whom and in whom and through whom we were made, the Son of God.

The soundtrack will suddenly give way to another song: "The Wedding Song of the Lamb."

"Hallelujah!
For our Lord God Almighty reigns.
Let us rejoice and be glad
and give him glory!
For the wedding of the Lamb has come,
and his bride has made herself ready."
(Rev. 19:6b-7)

And who knows, maybe it will be playing from a vinyl record! I do know this, we will be dancing and singing and moving to the grooving.

HOW THIS READER WORKS

. . . .

For the next seven weeks I will be leading you through a season of deep devotion to God by reading, singing, praying, and reflecting on the Songs (the Psalms). Each day begins with a psalm and is followed by a short reflection designed to spark your own rumination. I will not be giving you a lot of "things to do." Each day will call for a simple application: sing the song. That's it.

As always, the study of Scripture works best when other people are involved. I encourage you to engage this journey with a spouse or a friend or even better, a group of friends or couples. This journey is designed to help people have nonthreatening yet meaningful conversations about how the Holy Spirit is at work in one another's lives. So often we are reluctant to talk about God with other people, not because we do not know what to say, but because we have no idea how to say it. This guide will help with that.

The Use of YHWH in the Psalms

In the Hebrew Old Testament, there is a range of words used for God. The most frequent terms are God (a generic term for the Creator of the heavens and the earth—*El* or *Elohim* in the Hebrew); Lord (a title of sovereignty—*Adonai* in the Hebrew); and the personal, covenantal name for God (*YHWH* in Hebrew, known as the Tetragrammaton, or four consonants). The covenantal name (YHWH) was not to be pronounced in the Jewish tradition, and out of respect for that tradition, Bible translations normally render this covenantal name as LORD, in all caps, or Lord, using small caps. This is the pattern followed in the psalms contained in this book.

Navigating Meters and Tunes

The psalms for our daily readings have been carefully and artfully crafted into a metrical, poetic format known as a Psalter. Seedbed commissioned Dr. Timothy and Mrs. Julie Tennent to work these psalms into this time-tested format. We call it the Seedbed Psalter.

At the start of each psalm in this book *Soundtrack: A Forty-Day Playlist Through the Psalms*, you will find both the meter and several suggested tunes. Remember that the meter is simply the pattern of syllables in each line of the song (example: 87.87 means a line with eight syllables followed by a line with seven syllables, repeated throughout the song).

The meter then determines which tunes may be used to sing that particular hymn or song. You will see various tune suggestions listed. You may not recognize the names of these tunes, but if you hear them, many of them may sound familiar. To assist you, we have developed an online site where you may find all sorts of guidance and help with the actual singing of these

Psalms. We've even commissioned some musicians and worship leaders to provide musical accompaniment. Check out **soundtrack.seedbed.com** to access it all. (To experience the entire 150 Psalms in the Seedbed Psalter with lots of additional resourcing, visit **psalms.seedbed.com**.)

Try singing the psalms to different tunes. Some tunes are majestic and celebrative; others are somber and quiet; some are reflective and others are mournful. The mood of the psalm may be brought to life in different ways by different tunes, so this allows for variety and multiple ways in which a psalm may be sung.

Finally, you'll see numbers listed alongside the text of the psalm. These correspond with the verse numbers just as they are in the book of Psalms. This format helps us to remember that these metrical settings follow the actual text of the biblical psalm, and that the tune is simply a vehicle for the journey. Both the meter and the tune are meant to carry the message of the psalm into the deep places of the heart and soul; but the journey is ultimately in the text, not the music.

For Those Engaging This Reader Through the Season of Lent

For well more than a thousand years, under the guidance of the Holy Spirit, the church has set aside certain times to practice the rhythms of repentance and restoration—seasons of fasting followed by periods of feasting. The forty days of Lent are one of these seasons. If you are following this reader through Lent, begin on Ash Wednesday. If you are engaging the guide at another point in the year, any day will do.

Lent . . . the season the world's company of choc-olatiers loves to hate. How on earth have we managed to reduce Jesus' forty-day, fiercely conflicted fast in the desert to, "I'm going to give up chocolate for Lent"? Or in my case, "I'm going to give up the grande, five-pump, no-water chai latte with a shot of espresso"? I suppose it has merit, letting go of these small indulgences, but in my experience, it typically only ratchets up my focus on them. Fasting must lead to a bigger focus than the thing being fasted from.

Finding Our Focus, Grooving Our Gaze

The big idea of the forty days of Lent is not first and fore-most about fasting. It's about focus. We must covenant not to talk about our fasting, but about our focus. Focus on what? Jesus Christ, God's Son, the Savior, the Lord. Why? Because he is:

- the Word made flesh (John 1:14)
- the image of the invisible God (Col. 1:15)
- the exact representation of God's being (Heb. 1:3)
- the One who created all things and for whom all things were created (Col. 1:16 and Rev. 4:11)
- he who is before all things and in whom all things hold together (Col. 1:17)
- the author and perfecter of our faith (Heb. 12:2 NASB)

- he who was, and is, and is to come (Rev. 1:4, 8; 4:8)
- he who reconciled all things to himself by making peace through his blood shed on the cross (Col. 1:20)
- the light of the world (John 8:12)
- the bread of life (John 6:35)
- the way and the truth and the life (John 14:6)
- the gate (John 10:7, 9)
- the door (John 10:9 NASB)
- the resurrection and the life (John 11:25)
- the true vine (John 15:1)
- the One who, being in very nature God, did not consider equality with God something to be used to his own advantage, but made himself nothing (Phil. 2:6–7)
- the King who humbled himself and became obedient to death—even death on a cross (Phil. 2:8)
- he whom God highly exalted and gave the name that is above every name (Phil. 2:9)
- the One before whom every knee will bow and every tongue acknowledge that Jesus Christ is Lord, to the glory of God the Father (Phil. 2:10–11)
- the Alpha and the Omega, the First and the Last, the Beginning and the End (Rev. 22:13)
- he who is making all things new (Rev. 21:5 NASB)

Stretched out before you now are forty days of focus. At your hands are the Word of God and the Spirit of God. All that remains is the consecration of your attention to the Risen Lord Jesus Christ, the singer and songwriter of the ages. Get ready to turn up the music and sing your heart inside-out.

SOUNDTRACK

How the Grande, Five-Pump, No-Water Chai Latte with a Shot of Espresso Works

. . . .

PSALM 6

TALLIS CANON, ROCKINGHAM OLD, or HAMBURG   88.88 L.M.
Words by Julie Tennent based on Psalm 6

1   O LORD, in anger don't rebuke,
     In wrath, don't chide or turn from me.
2   Have mercy, LORD, for I am faint,
     My very bones in agony.

3   Come heal me, LORD, my anguished soul
     cries out, "How long, O LORD, how long?"
4   Deliver me, and save me, LORD—
     Your steadfast love remains my song.

5   No one can praise You from the grave,
     Nor mention You when they are dead.
6   I groan all day, all night I weep;
     My tears now drench and flood my bed.

7   My eyes grow weak with sorrow and
    they fail because of all my foes.
8   Depart from me, you evil ones!
    The LORD has heard my cries and woes.

9   The LORD in mercy heard my cry;
    Receives my prayer before His face.
10 My enemies will be dismayed,
    And turn back, shamed and in disgrace.

Consider This . . .

Here the psalmist teaches us a song of deliverance.
Notice how the singer holds together two divergent realities throughout the song. While struggle and agony will
not release the singer, the singer will not let go of the
love of God. Were we to map the genome of the Psalms,
one of the primary strands of DNA would be this insepa-
rable, discordant bond between the deep inner pain of
a thousand circumstances of people, and the deeper,
softer, yet stronger melody of the Deliverer. See it at
work in this verse:

> Come heal me, LORD, my anguished soul
> cries out, "How long, O LORD, how long?"
> Deliver me, and save me, LORD—
> Your steadfast love remains my song.

Though I can't prove it, my strong hunch is that Jesus
sang through the 150 Psalms throughout his forty days
in the wilderness. He sang them throughout his life, right
up to Song 22 from the cross. These songs simultaneously acclimate us to the realities of being human and

the reality of the love of God. And the truth? I can't know one without the other.

The songs and stories of every age aspire to transport us to some illusory place of pain-free life where we write our own prescriptions and where we call the shots and control the outcomes. (And isn't that what the tempter was up to both in Eden and with Jesus in the wilderness and later at Gethsemane?) This is the battle. Over and over and over the psalmist takes us straight to the front lines. It's a hard fight, but it's the good fight, and it's the way of Jesus. And because he won, we will win.

If I'm honest, I don't really want to go there. Something about that grande, five-pump, no-water chai latte with a shot of espresso can keep reality at bay for a little while. The insatiable strategy of small indulgences works like that.

Ask Yourself. Share with Another.

On a scale of one to ten, with ten being the highest, how much do you turn to the practice of small indulgences (emotional eating and drinking) to get through the rough spots in life?

DAY 2

How the Psalms Work More Like Orange Juice Concentrate than Simply Orange

. . . .

PSALM 90

ST. ANNE   86.86 C.M.
Words by Julie Tennent based on Psalm 90

1   Lord, You have been our dwelling place, through
       generations all;
    From age to age, our hiding place; our refuge whom
       we call.

2   Before the mountains came to be, or earth sprang
       from Your word;
    From everlasting to all time, You are the only God.

3   You turn men back to dust and say, "Return, O sons
       of men";
    For dust we are, to dust return; we go to dust again.

4   A thousand years are merely like a day within
       Your sight;

A day soon gone, or like a watch that passes in
the night.

5   We're swept away as in death's sleep; like new grass
in the morn;
6   Though it sprouts up with morning light, by dusk it's
dry and worn.

7   For by Your anger we're consumed; in terror at
Your wrath;
8   You've set our sins before You, and Your light reveals
their path.

9   Our days pass quickly in Your wrath; years like a sigh
are past;
10 Our length of days are seventy, or eighty if
strength last.

And yet their span's with trouble filled, and sorrow
marks our way;
Days quickly pass and soon are gone; and we just
fly away.

11 Who knows the power of Your wrath? It's great as fear
You're due!
12 Teach us to number right our days and gain Your
wisdom true.

13 Relent, O Lord! How long till You have mercy on
Your saints?
14 Come satisfy us in the morn with love that
never faints.

Then we will sing for joy, and will be glad for all
our days;
15 O make us glad as many days as we've known
troubled ways.

16   May Your deeds and Your works be shown unto Your
       servants all;
       Your splendor to their children and to those who on
       You call.

17   May God's good favor rest on us; our work before
       Him stand.
       Yes, Lord our God, establish firm the work of our
       own hands.

Consider This . . .

Growing up, we didn't have the present-day luxury of
bottled juices such as Simply Orange. We actually got
those little cans out of the freezer, often thawing them
overnight, and mixed the contents with water to make
our orange juice. The cans contained an ingredient
known as *concentrate*, a thick, syrupy, profoundly orange
substance. I used to love prying the lid off early before
breakfast and sneaking a small spoonful of the stuff into
my mouth. It produced a bit of a mouth-explosion effect
of goodness. But who could take more than a spoonful?
The taste vividly remains with me.

That's what the Psalms are like and how they work.
They gather up all of the glorious details from Scripture
of the character of God and all of the dastardly depths of
the human condition and combine them into a powerful
concentrate. We can only take about a spoonful at a
time. And that's okay, because over time they mingle
with the water that is our lives and result in something

unexpectedly good. At times the concentrate is so strong that it's bitter; at other times it tastes pleasantly sweet.

Song 90 gives us a massively concentrated contrast between the incomprehensible infiniteness of God and the frail finiteness of human beings:

> Before the mountains came to be, or earth sprang
>   from Your word;
> From everlasting to the same, You, only You, are God.
>
> You turn men back to dust and say, "Return, O sons
>   of men";
> For dust we are, to dust return; we go to dust again.

We need this concentrated reminder. As for me, "dust, dust, dust, dust. You, only You, are God."

Something about actually singing these songs brings out the fullness of their taste. And yes, it is a bit of an acquired taste. It will take time. Just sing this one today.

Ask Yourself. Share with Another.

Can you think of a story or situation in your past when you realized your own frailty and finiteness? What might it mean to think of yourself as made of dirt yet filled with the breath of God? How do those two realities work together? Or not?

Sing it at soundtrack.seedbed.com

DAY 3

Depression Is Normal;
It Needs a Soundtrack

· ·

PSALM 42

MORNING SONG   86.86 C.M.
Words by Julie Tennent based on Psalm 42

1   As the deer pants for water clear, so my soul thirsts
for You;
2   My soul thirsts for the living God; when can I meet
with You?

3   My tears have been my food all through the day and
through the night;
While men mock me and say all day, "Where is your
God of might?"

4   These things I do remember, Lord, as I pour out
my soul:
How I went with the multitude into the house of God.

I led the great procession with a shout of joy
and song;
With thanksgiving I went among the festive,
joyful throng.

5   Why are you so downcast, my soul? Why so disturbed
       in me?
    Put hope in God—I'll praise Him yet; my Savior God
       is He!

6   My soul is downcast within me, so I remember You;
    From land along the Jordan, heights of Hermon,
       Mizar, too.

7   Deep calls to deep within the roar of Your
       great waterfalls;
    Your waves and breakers swept o'er me; they flood
       me without pause.

8   By day the LORD directs His love, His steadfast love
       to me;
    At night His song is with me still—my prayer to God
       will be.

9   I say to God my Rock, "O why have You forgotten me?
    Why must I mourn all day oppressed by the vile enemy?

10 My bones do suffer mortal pain; my foes taunt me
       all day;
    "Where is your God?" they mock with scorn; "Where
       is your God?" they say.

11 Why are you so downcast, my soul? Why so disturbed
       in me?
    Put hope in God—I'll praise Him yet; my Savior God
       is He!

Consider This . . .

Depression is a normal part of being human. The Psalms
present depression as par for the course in the human

experience. The singer instructs us in the counterintuitive practice of embracing depression rather than trying to escape it.

Song 42 is not a sweet praise chorus about a thirsty deer. It is the desperate cry of a depressed soul. The singer literally can't stop crying. The promising path of past success has come to a screeching halt, a dead end with no way out. The Quakers would speak of this almost universal human experience as "way closing." Depression can be expected in the wake of way closing. Frantic efforts to make way open again will only make it worse.

The psalm shows us the contours of an unlikely remedy: singing. Here's the shape of the song. We must become gut-level honest about our interior conditions, which requires that we ask our souls the piercing question: *Soul, why are you so depressed?* And we may need some help from a friend, pastor, or counselor to answer it. Medication can be very helpful in such times, but it is not a strategy. We must learn to grieve our losses and even mourn and cry in this stuck place. We must learn to pour out our souls to God.

Finally, we must cease anchoring our hopes in "way open," which so often in our minds is just another idealistic reconstruction of the past. We must follow the song to the bridge. What makes a good song great isn't the chorus. It's the bridge. The bridge leads us out of the depths of sadness and into the depths of Love, where we find that "way" is not some new opportunity or direction—Way is God!

> By day the Lord directs His love, His steadfast love to me;
> At night His song my comfort is; my prayer to God will be.

Depression is normal. It can take time to pass through. Way is God. Never stop singing.

Ask Yourself. Share with Another.

Many people suffer with a condition called "low-grade" depression. It's not necessarily diagnosable but it's there. Pardon the image, but it's sort of like a constipation of the soul. Do you get what I'm talking about? You feel neither alive nor dead, but the dim "blah" of in-between. Does this sound familiar to your own experience? Sometimes just naming it can help. Let the song lead you in praying through it.

Sing it at soundtrack.seedbed.com

DAY 4

How the Psalms Get Beyond Anger Management

PSALM 43

MORNING SONG   86.86 C.M.
Words by Julie Tennent based on Psalm 43

1   O vindicate and plead my cause, O God, against
      the foe;
    Come rescue me from wicked men, a nation vile
      and low.

2   You are my stronghold and my God; why do You
      reject me?
    Why must I mourn all day oppressed by the
      vile enemy?

3   Send forth Your light and send Your truth, and let
      them guide me well.
    O let them bring me to Your mount, the place where
      You do dwell.

4   Then I'll go to God's altar—God, my joy and
      my delight;
    And I will praise You with the harp, O God, my God,
      my light.

5   Why are you so downcast, my soul? Why so disturbed
      in me?
    Put hope in God—I'll praise Him yet; my Savior God
      is He!

Consider This . . .

Jesus instructed us to love our enemies and to pray for those who persecute us (Matt. 5.44), which sounds good . . . until I actually have an enemy. Then it's a pretty big stretch. Song 43 models a more doable strategy. At least it's a starting place. The singer decides to take the battle not to the throat of the enemy but to the heart of God.

Though he wrote these words in another context, John Calvin's words ring true throughout the Psalms: "It is God with whom we have to deal."[2] Whether our situation is for better or worse, for richer or poorer, in sickness or in health, the Psalms always redirect our attention, affections, angst, and emotions to God alone.

Are you facing an irreconcilable injustice somewhere in your life today? Does it seem your enemies are prevailing? Do you need to be vindicated in some situation? Is there a painful chasm in your marriage or a divisive feud in your community? How about an incomprehensible tragedy? In the face of well-intentioned people (often pastors) who console with words like, "God has a reason for this," or, "God is allowing this to happen for his glory," today's song and many more like it teach a different set of rules for divine engagement. And there's really only one rule: it is God with whom we have to deal.

Don't hold back. Cry out for vindication. Sing out your angst to God against your enemies. Not only is this a healthy way of dealing with our problems, but it is a holy way. Frankly, it is the only way if we are ever to arrive at a true place of loving our enemies.

It is God with whom we have to deal.

There's something about singing these words (over time) that takes them to a whole new level. It's like going from black and white to full Technicolor. Sing this one now.

Ask Yourself. Share with Another.

Do you carry around anger or angst at people or situations? Do you tend to express it to them? Or do you have a lot of angry fantasy conversations with them in your head? If this describes you, chances are you are a passive-aggressive person. What is a better strategy?

Sing it at soundtrack.seedbed.com

DAY 5

What to Do with a Psalm When You're Just Not Feeling It

· ·

PSALM 44

FOUNDATION or ST. DENIO   11.11.11.11
Words by Julie Tennent based on Psalm 44

1   O God, we have heard what our fathers have told,
    What You did in their days, days glor'ous of old.
2   With Your hand You drove out the nations and gave
    our fathers their land, crushed all foes in the grave.

3   It was not by sword that they took all the land;
    Their arm brought no vict'ry—it was by Your hand.
    Your right hand, Your arm, and the light of Your face,
    You loved them so truly, and showed them Your grace.

4   O Lord, You're my God, and You are my great King;
    And vict'ries for Jacob You plan and You bring.
5   Through You we push back, enemies we depose;
    Through Your name we trample upon all our foes.

6   I trust not my own bow, nor sword for my fame;
7   For You give the vict'ry; put our foes to shame.

8   In God we will boast all throughout the day long;
    And we'll praise Your name, Lord, forever in song.

9   But now You reject us and humble us, too;
    Our armies go out, but no longer with You.
10 You made us retreat, as the enemy closed,
    And we have been plundered by vi-o-lent foes.

11 Now we are de-vour-ed like sheep that are lost;
    You let us be scattered and helplessly tossed.
12 You sold us, Your people, and nothing did gain;
    You gave up Your people for others to reign.

13 We're now a reproach to our neighbors and friends;
    The scorn and derision of them never ends.
14 You've made us a byword among nations all;
    They shake their heads at us, and mockingly call.

15 Disgrace is before me throughout all the day;
    My face must be covered; shame won't go away.
16 They taunt and revile me; reproach never ends;
    Because of my foes who are bent on revenge.

17 Now all this has happened, though we had been true;
    We broke not Your cov'nant; did not forget You.
18 Our hearts had not turned back; our feet had not strayed;
19 You crushed us in darkness; a jackal's haunt made.

20 If we had forgotten the name of our God,
    Or spread out our hand to a false, foreign god;
21 Would God not have seen it, since He knows our heart?
22 For Your sake we face death, like sheep torn apart.

23 Awake, Lord! Why sleep? Don't reject us again.
24 Why hide Your face? When will our misery end?
25 We're brought down to dust, our life's flung to
        the ground;
26 Rise up now and help us! Let Your love abound!

Consider This . . .

I remember years ago the first time I walked into a Gold's Gym. The sheer number of different weight-lifting machines and exercise stations stunned me. I thought to myself, *Who could do all this?* In one of my early novice workouts, I decided to try out every machine and station. I think I took the next year off from the gym. Seriously, I discovered muscles I never knew I had. I learned it would take a structured approach over a long period of time to develop my atrophied muscular system. In that season of my life, I grew stronger than ever before, and it improved every aspect of my health and wellness.

Writing in the latter part of the fourth century, Ambrose, the archbishop of Milan, in his commentary on the Psalms, described them as "a gymnasium which is open for all souls to use, where the different psalms are like different exercises set out before him. In that gymnasium, in that stadium of virtue, he can choose the exercises that will train him best to win the victor's crown."[3]

When I come to a psalm like today's, I've got to be honest; I'm just not feeling it. All the angst of being forsaken, forgotten, and rejected for no apparent reason is just not my present experience. It's kind of like what happened to me in the gym over time. Little by little my exercise regimen got smaller and smaller and also much less diverse. I went for my favorite lifting machines that strengthened my already developed muscles. When it came to the cable crossover exercises, it got easier and easier to "skip that one today."

Ambrose nailed it in his word on the Psalms. As it is in the gym, so it is with the Psalms. Think of the soul as a type of muscular system. The muscles I exercise will strengthen. The muscles I neglect will atrophy. The trouble with the soul is I have no mirror to assess my condition. It takes a real, live situation to expose the soul. If I am not working out with psalms like today's text, the muscles will simply not be there when the time comes.

Song 44 is a long way from Song 23. "The Lord is my Shepherd" is in a completely different part of the gym than, "Yet now we face death, and like sheep we're disowned."

I am going to address you as a maturing believer. Do the exercise. It doesn't matter if you feel it. Sing it now.

Ask Yourself. Share with Another.

Can you remember a time when you did not have the inner strength to deal with a person or situation in the way you wanted? How might you exercise and strengthen that part of your soul?

Sing it at soundtrack.seedbed.com

DAY 6

Understanding the Psalms as a Sing-Along Rather than a Solo Performance

PSALM 7

PENITENTIA, MORECAMBE, or NATIONAL HYMN   10.10.10.10
Words by Timothy Tennent based on Psalm 7

1   O LORD, my God, in You I refuge take,
     Save me from those who would pursue my life.
2   Like a strong lion they would tear and shake,
     Leaving no help in all my painful strife.

3   If, LORD my God, I'm guilty in Your sight,
     If there is guilt and sin upon my hand,
4   If I've robbed friends, or evil done in spite,
5   May my life be cast down at Your command.

6   Arise, O LORD, in anger right and mete,
     Your fury rage against my enemies;
7   Awake, my God, rise to Your judgment seat,
     Let the assembly know of Your decrees.

8   The righteous LORD, He judges all the earth;
     Judge me, O LORD, by Your true righteousness.

Vindicate me and judge me by my worth,
According to my life of faithfulness.

9　O God, you search the minds and hearts of men,
You end the violence of the wicked ones;
Oh, bring all sin to its appointed end!
And do establish all Your righteous ones.

10　My shield is God who saves those in the right;
11　He is indignant o'er the sins of men.
12　If we won't turn, His sword is raised to fight;
His bow is bent, and poised to strike again.

13　He has prepared His deadly weapons now;
He makes His arrows with their fiery shafts.
14　The wicked man conceives an evil vow,
Bringing to birth those sins and lies he crafts!

15　He digs a pit and makes it big and round,
But he falls in the pit that he has made.
16　His mischief turns, upon him does rebound;
Violence comes down on him and he's betrayed.

17　I will give thanks which to the LORD is due;
His righteousness is over everything;
I will sing praises to the name most true—
The LORD Most High, His glories I will sing.

Consider This . . .

It never would have occurred to me to sing these lines:

The righteous LORD, He judges all the earth;
Judge me, O LORD, by Your true righteousness.
Remember me and judge me by my worth,
According to my life of faithfulness.

Around 123 songs later in this same songbook they have us singing these lyrics, "If you, O Lᴏʀᴅ, kept a record of sins, who could stand?" (Ps. 130:3).

The only person who could legitimately sing Song 7 is Jesus Christ himself. The amazing thing is he not only sang Psalm 7, he sang it for us; and he did so in such a way that we can now sing it with him.

Because Jesus is our righteousness, we can boldly sing, "Judge me, O Lord, by Your true righteousness." We are not confident in our own righteousness or faithfulness; only in his. What a gift!

When we sing these 150 Songs, let us remember we join our voices with both the singer and songwriter, the Son of God, Jesus Christ. Thank God. All of the Psalms are yes and amen in and through and because of him.

Ask Yourself. Share with Another.

Have you come to the place where you realize your righteousness will never measure up? Or are you still trying to measure up? Do you really understand (at the level of personal experience) that Jesus measures up for you?

Sing it at soundtrack.seedbed.com

How I Got a Splinter in My Soul and How I Got It Out

. . . .

PSALM 39

MORNING SONG or DUNDEE   86.86 C.M.
Words by Julie Tennent based on Psalm 39

1   I said, "I will watch all my ways, and keep my tongue
      from sin;
    I'll put a muzzle on my mouth while with such
      wicked men."

2   But while I silent was and still, not even
      speaking good;
    The anguish in my soul increased, though try as best
      I could.

3   My heart grew hotter within me, as, thinking one
      by one
    of all my troubles, the fire burned; then I spoke with
      my tongue:

4   "Show me, O Lord, what is my life, the number of
      my days;
    Make me to know how fast it flies; how fleeting are
      my days.

5   For You have made life but a breath; my days but a
        short span;
    My years as nothing before You, a mere breath is
        each man.

6   And phantom-like we go about, we scurry all in vain;
    We heap up wealth, yet know not who will end up
        with our gain.

7   But now, Lord, what do I look for? My only hope's
        in You.
8   Save me from my transgressions, and the scorn of
        fools subdue.

9   I'm silent, and keep my mouth closed, for You all this
        have done.
10 Remove Your scourge from me, for by Your hand
        I'm overcome.

11 For You rebuke and discipline all men for all their sin;
    And You consume our wealth—it flies, like moths
        before the wind.

12 O hear my prayer, Lord, listen, as for help to You I cry;
    Don't be deaf to my weeping—like a foreigner am I.

    I'm like a stranger to You, as my fathers were before;
13 Turn Your gaze from me; let me smile, before I am
        no more."

Consider This . . .

I remember as a child, somewhere in that season around
the so-called "age of accountability," I got a splinter in
my soul. Reading my Bible one morning, I came across
Matthew 16:26: "For what will it profit a man if he gains

the whole world and forfeits his soul? Or what will a man give in exchange for his soul?" (NASB).

These words bothered me. They still do. They set up a stark contrast I have never managed to get past. On the one hand: the whole world. On the other hand: my soul. I so want to dwell somewhere in the decision-less middle. I want a life overflowing with monetary wealth and I want a soul filled with God. The text tells me I must decide on one or the other. As a kid, I somehow knew the splinter of this saying would pulsate with nagging pain until I aimed my life in one of these two directions. It was clear to me. These roads led to two completely different destinations, and one of those would look like great gain and yet be complete loss. Little did I know at the time how these words would stick in my soul like a tiny shard of wood even to the present day. As an adult I now know this is not a one-time transaction. It's an everyday decision.

Though there's a lot going on in Song 39, these stanzas strike me as the heart of it:

> "Show me, O LORD, what is my life, the number of my days;
> Make me to know how fast it flies; how fleeting are my days.
>
> For You have made life but a breath; my days but a short span;
> My years as nothing before You, a mere breath is each man.
>
> And phantom-like we go about, we scurry all in vain;
> We heap up wealth, yet know not who will end up with our gain."

It's a prayer for the big picture. The song lifts me out of the messy melody of today and shows me the music of a lifetime. How often am I getting to a place where I can see the whole score and grasp the shortness of the soundtrack of my life? This is the agenda of Song 39.

So what does it profit a person to gain the whole world and forfeit his or her soul?

Again, the devil took him to a very high mountain and showed him all the kingdoms of the world and their splendor. "All this I will give you," he said, "if you will bow down and worship me." Jesus said to him, "Away from me, Satan! For it is written: 'Worship the Lord your God, and serve him only.'" (Matt. 4:8–10)

I bet he was singing Song 39. Give it a shot today. Sing it.

Ask Yourself. Share with Another.

This is usually where the proverbial rubber meets the road. Have you come to realize the major players competing for top spot in your deepest self? One of the upsides of having everything is the deep, holy discontent it can produce in the pit of your soul. Feel it?

Sing it at soundtrack.seedbed.com

DAY 8

Thoughts on Sin Cancer and Chemotherapy for the Soul

. . . .

PSALM 32

BEACH SPRING or EBENEZER   87.87 D
Words by Julie Tennent based on Psalm 42

1   Blessed is the man whose sin is covered over by
        the Lord;
      Whose transgressions are forgiven, whose guilt God
        does not record.
2   Blessed is the man whose sin the LORD does not count
        against him;
      In whose spirit there is not found cruel deceit deep
        down within.

3   When I held my sin inside me, and kept silent in
        my way,
      Then my bones grew weak and wasted through
        my groaning all the day.
4   For Your hand was heavy on me; day and night, my
        strength did lapse;
      Sapped away as in the heat of summer's hot,
        lethargic grasp.

5   Then I told You of my sin and did not hide iniquity;

I said, "I'll confess my trespass"—You forgave, purged
    guilt from me.
6   Therefore, let the godly pray to You while You may
        still be found;
    Surely waters will not reach me, when with might they
        surge around.

7   For You are my place of hiding, You protect me from
        all strife;
    And with songs of Your deliv'rance, You surround and
        keep my life.
8   "I will teach and will instruct you in the way that you
        should go;
    I will counsel and watch o'er you, the right path to you
        I'll show."

9   Don't be like the horse or mule who do not
        understand at all;
    They're controlled by bit and bridle, or won't come
        when you do call.
10   Many are woes of the wicked, but the LORD's
        unfailing love
11   does surround the ones who trust Him. Sing! Rejoice
        in God above!

Consider This . . .

Anytime someone we love gets diagnosed with cancer, we
all have three major sequential questions: Is it curable?
Has it spread? Following surgery to remove cancer, we
ask the third question: Did they get it all?

One of the things I appreciate about Song 32 is the
way it characterizes sin. So often we limit sin to categories

of morality, of good and evil. It's actually more than that. Sin is sickness. Sin is the cancer of the soul. It is fiercely malignant and unyieldingly terminal. Sin cancer gets all of us in the end, for sin is to death as free radicals are to cancer. The even bigger devastation of sin cancer is that it can kill us before we die. Take another look at the second stanza in today's reading.

The good news: there is a remedy for cancer. The cure is confession. It has a 100 percent cure rate.

I used to think confession was a form of admitting what a loser I am. Somewhere along the way, grace taught me better. Here's my present working definition of confession: agreeing with God about what is true. I confess that Jesus is Lord. True. I confess that I am a sinner. True. It is an agreement made at the core of the core of who I am.

See the third stanza in today's reading. Confession is not admission. Confession is not self-shaming. Confession is simple honesty about what is true about us. "Lord Jesus, I confess that I was unkind to my wife this morning. That was sin." Confession is simple honesty before God that will lead to a life of integrity before others.

Song 32 teaches us that unconfessed sin is like a cancer of the soul. It eats us alive. These forty days provide an open door to walk through as concerns our honesty before God. Here's a way in. Begin with a form of the most ancient prayer of all, *Kyrie eleison*: "Lord, have mercy." Consider engaging a form of the prayer known as The Jesus Prayer: "Lord Jesus Christ, Son of God, have mercy on me, a sinner."

We will revisit this, but for now, just take it on like a mantra. Say it all the time, just under your breath. The specificity of confession will come. Consider this as though it were a round of chemotherapy. Drip. Drip. Drip.

And don't forget. It's time to sing again.

Ask Yourself. Share with Another.

Do you have trouble owning The Jesus Prayer? Why might that be the case?

DAY 9

How a Song Can Be a Shield (or Why St. Patrick's Day Must Become about More than Green Beer)

· ·

PSALM 86

ST. ANNE, NEW BRITAIN, or SALZBURG   86.86 C.M.
Words by Julie Tennent based on Psalm 86

1   Hear me, O Lord, and answer me; I'm poor and in
     great need;
2   Come, guard my life; You are my God. Save me! I trust
     in Thee.

3   Have mercy, Lord, I call to You all day with my
     heart full;
4   Restore my joy, for unto You, O Lord, I lift my soul.

5   For You are good and gracious, Lord, and ready
     to forgive;
     And You abound in love to all who call on You to live.

6   O hear my prayer, Lord, as I cry for mercy unto Thee;
7   When trouble comes, I call to You, for You will
     answer me.

8   Among the gods there's none like You; for only You
       are Lord;
     And neither are there deeds which can compare at all
       with Yours.

9   All nations You have made will come and
       worship rev'rently,
     They will bring glory to Your name; O Lord, they'll
       worship Thee.

10   For You alone are great, O Lord, and marv'lous are
       Your deeds;
     For You alone are God, O Lord; Your glory all exceeds.

11   Teach me Your way, LORD, and I'll walk in Your truth all
       my days;
     Give me an undivided heart to fear Your name always.

12   O Lord my God, with all my heart, to You I will
       give praise;
     And I will glorify Your name forever and always.

13   Great is the love You have toward me; Your love that
       acts to save;
     You have delivered me from Sheol; from the depths of
       the grave.

14   The arrogant attack me, God—a band of ruthless ones;
     They seek my life with no regard for You and all
       You've done.

15   But You, O Lord, are merciful and full of graciousness;
     To anger, slow; abundant in both love and faithfulness.

16   O turn to me with mercy, for my hope on You
       is stayed;
     Grant strength unto Your servant, save the son of
       Your handmaid.

17   Give me a sign of good from You, so that my foes
       will see
     and be ashamed; for You, O Lᴏʀᴅ, do help and
       comfort me.

Consider This . . .

In North America, the month of March offers all sorts
of variety. There's the NCAA basketball tournament and
March Madness. Then there's Lent. And, of course, somewhere along the way March became associated with wind
and flying kites. March 3 is the feast day of celebration in
the Anglican Church for John and Charles Wesley. And
don't forget to beware the ominous Ides of March, that
fateful day marking the assassination of Julius Caesar.
Tucked away in March we also find St. Patrick's Day.

     The interesting thing about St. Patrick's Day is
how it has become about wearing green and drinking
green beer and four-leaf clovers and parades and virtually everything else but Saint Patrick himself. It seems
like our little green friend, Master Yoda, should at least
get honorable mention on St. Patty's day, doesn't it?
Nevertheless, I think the best way we could possibly cele-
brate St. Patrick's Day would be for all of the followers
of Jesus to walk out into the streets at high noon and
together declare the prayer that has come to be known
as "the Breastplate of St. Patrick." It would be an awe-
inspiring thing to behold; the body of Christ collectively
taking up her shield of faith. Then we would move on
to a stadium-styled liturgy of Ephesians 6 and Paul's

admonition to put on the full armor of God . . . but I'm getting carried away now.

As with so much of history, the Breastplate of St. Patrick has been reduced to its sound bites by now. I'm talking about tracking out the whole shebang—witches, smiths, wizards, poison, drowning, burning, and all. Nothing like this ancient prayer brings faith to the fore as a shield. And this is what faith is: a real, live shield; not a sentimental hopefulness, but a Spirit-fueled, tangible reality. Faith is palpable protection. You know it when you see it.

It brings me to Song 86. As I sing it through, it strikes me that the singer here is armoring up with a great shield of faith. Consider the first two lines:

> Hear me, O LORD, and answer me;
>   I'm poor and in great need;
> Come, guard my life; You are my God.
>   Save me! I trust in Thee.

The song goes on to pile on layer after layer of the character, history, attributes, and nature of the Almighty. Promise rises up into prophecy, and protection becomes a song of deliverance.

The great irony of a shield of faith is that it makes the bearer look even more vulnerable. (Get a picture of David in your mind in his bout with the giant.) The shield will appear deceptively invisible to the enemy. The great relief of the shield of faith is the way it graces us with the power to lay down all our tired strategies of self-protection. Self-protection in exchange for God's protection. It's a pretty good deal.

It's time to sing it. A song can only become a shield if you sing it. Try the tune "New Britain." It's only the most popular melody in the history of history. Hint: "Amazing Grace."

Ask Yourself. Share with Another.

Is faith really a shield for you? Can you recount a situation where it was?

How the Underdog Wins in the End

PSALM 13

BEACH SPRING   87.87 D
Words by Julie Tennent based on Psalm 13

1   How long, LORD, will You forget me?
    How long will You hide Your face?
2   How long, LORD, will this depression
    grip my soul in its embrace?
    How long will this dreadful sorrow
    pierce my heart all night and day?
    How long will my soul's attacker
    be exalted o'er my way?

3   Look on me, LORD, come and answer;
    Light my eyes, lest death approach.
4   Lest my enemy claim vict'ry
    and my foes gloat in reproach.
5   But I trust Your lovingkindness
    and my heart shall yet rejoice;
6   For the LORD has been good to me,
    I will sing with heart and voice.

Consider This . . .

Every time the doors were open, she was there. She always arrived early, never missing an opportunity to be there. And like clockwork, this small, frail widow presented her case before the towering, distant judge, appealing for mercy, for justice, for relief, and for vindication from her enemy. And every day, like clockwork, the callous judge dismissed her pleadings. Despite the ever-mounting despair, she would never give up. For her it wasn't "if," but "when." Her only question seemed to be: How long? Finally, one day everything changed. Finally, the judge, worn down as dripping water wears on a rock, granted her plea. He simply wanted to be done with her. Widow wins. Case closed.

The moral to the story? Try harder? Never give up? Sort of, but not really. Jesus told this story to his disciples so they would "always pray and never give up" (Luke 18:1 NLT). But we so easily miss the point if we stop there. We readily translate the story into something like this: the answers to my pleas for help depend on the degree of my persistence in prayer. *Wrong!* The real truth behind the story: never give up, because the God to whom you pray is nothing whatsoever like the judge in the story. God always sees, always hears, always cares, always responds, always loves, and always wins—even if it takes a while; and sometimes it will. It's not our persistence that gets it done in the end. It's the unwavering, unfaltering, unfailing, unflinching love of God in Jesus Christ that gets it done. What fuels the persistence Jesus speaks of is not our dogged self-determination, but an unstoppable faith in this kind of God! Hang on . . . what's that music I hear in the distance?

Song 13 is the soundtrack of the widow's story. She probably sang it every time she climbed those court-house steps. Can you hear her frail voice singing those last verses as her hand once again reached for the door?

> But I trust Your lovingkindness
> and my heart shall yet rejoice;
> For the LORD has been good to me,
> I will sing with heart and voice.

That's the truth about underdogs. They never stop singing.

Ask Yourself. Share with Another.

Am I really growing in my confidence in God or do I still believe self-confidence is the preferred path? It can mean the difference between faith and faking it.

Sing it at soundtrack.seedbed.com

DAY 11

The Song That Makes People Reject God

PSALM 137

MORNING SONG   86.86 C.M.
Words by Julie Tennent based on Psalm 137

1   By rivers of cruel Babylon, there we sat down
and wept;
When we remembered you, Zion—our home we'll
not forget.

2   Upon the trees we hung our harps, for they
demanded song.

3   Our captors, with triumphant scorn, said, "Sing songs
of Zion."

4   But how can we the LORD's song sing within a
foreign land?

5   If I forget Jerusalem, let skill leave my right hand.

6   May my tongue cleave to my mouth's roof, if I do
not recall;
If I don't praise Jerusalem, my chief joy above all.

7   Remember, LORD, all Edom's sons who
razed Jerusalem;

Who said, "Tear down, tear down its walls unto
    its foundation."

8   O daughter of doomed Babylon, you devastated one;
    How bless'd will be the one who pays to you as you
        have done.

9   How bless-ed ever will he be, who thus ends
        your cruelty;
    Who dashes e'en your little ones upon the rocks justly.

Consider This . . .

Song 137 may be the most difficult passage in all of the
Bible. Here we find Israel robbed of virtually everything
but their breath (and many had been robbed of that).
After marching them out of their homes and into the
corpulent abyss of Babylonian exile, after losing everything they had, after it got worse than the worst could
have possibly been—it was then their captors demanded
them to sing the songs of Zion. This scene offers a truly
unthinkable moment. It was for this moment they wrote
an almost unsingable song—Song 137.

How bless-ed ever will he be, who thus ends your
    cruelty;
Who dashes e'en your little ones upon the rocks
    justly.

Song 137 is one of the ten imprecatory psalms (7, 35,
55, 58, 59, 69, 79, 109, 137, and 139). What is an imprecatory psalm? It's when the songwriter calls down napalm
from heaven on his enemies' heads—and in the case of

137, on their children. It's a prayer and plea to God for immediate, unmitigated justice.

Julie Tennent, one of the creators of the Seedbed Psalter, from which our daily texts have come, has written some helpful guidance on how to approach these psalms. It's titled, "We're Not Supposed to Sing Those Psalms, Are We?" It can be found in the bonus tracks section of this book (a.k.a. the Appendix).

Why is this so important? These psalms, and this one in particular, pose significant barriers to faith for many people in today's world. Who hasn't had the argument thrown at them that they want no part of a God whose inspired Word involves the murder of other people's children? As ambassadors of Christ we must learn to help others, many of who are in desperate need of the grace of God, to navigate these troubled waters. We must learn to approach these conversations not as God's lawyers, but as witnesses to his character.

If you are up for it, try singing what feels like an unsingable song.

Ask Yourself. Share with Another.

Have you ever had to deal with this particular passage of Scripture? How did you do it? Do you need a better approach?

Sing it at soundtrack.seedbed.com

DAY 12

How Psalms Help Us Deal with Our Inner Gangster

PSALM 59

KINGSFOLD   86.86 C.M. D
Words by Julie Tennent based on Psalm 59

1   Deliver me, O God, from those that are my enemies;
    Protect me from all those who do rise up to
        threaten me.

2   Deliver me from wicked ones who do evil again;
    And save me from the wickedness of those
        bloodthirsty men.

3   See how they lie in wait for me! They fiercely
        do combine
    against me, Lord; they do conspire for no offense
        of mine.

4   I've done no wrong, yet they in wait are ready to
        seize me;
    Arise to help me, Lord my God, look on my plight
        and see!

5   Awake, Almighty Lord of hosts, O God of Israel,
    Arouse Yourself to punish all that wickedly rebel.

6   At ev'ning they go to and fro; they make great noise
        and sound;
     They snarl like dogs and prowl about the city
        all around.

7   See what they spew out from their mouths; for in their
        lips are swords;
     And they say, "Who can possibly hear any of
        our words?"
8   But You, O Lord will laugh at them, and at the
        nations scoff;
9   My strength, I'll watch and wait for You, my fortress
        and my rock.

10   My loving God goes before me; He'll let me gloat
        and see
     the end of all those wicked ones, who mock and
        slander me.
11   But do not kill them, Lord, our shield, or people
        will forget;
     By Thy strong power bring them down, and make
        them wander yet.

12   And for the sins which their mouths speak, the words
        their lips let fly,
     Let them be caught in their own pride, because they
        curse and lie.
13   Consume them in Your wrath, O Lord; consume till
        they're no more.
     It will be known to ends of earth that Jacob's God
        is Lord.

14   At ev'ning they go to and fro; they make great noise
        and sound;
     They snarl like dogs, and prowl about the city
        all around.

15   They wander, searching for their food; and if
        not satisfied,
      They howl like dogs and prowl around, and don't care
        how they've lied.

16   But I'll sing of Your strength, O God; at dawn Your
        love I'll praise;
      For You're my fortress, refuge, and my tow'r in
        troubled days.
17   O God, You are my strength, and I sing praises
        unto You;
      O God, You are my fortress, full of lovingkindness true.

Consider This . . .

Back-to-back imprecatory psalms. So can we cut the
fancy language and just call it what it is? Song 59 and a
series of others of its ilk are the gangster psalms of the
Bible. They are the melodies of revenge; the "I'm going to
make you sorry for the day you were born" songs. Picture
Clint Eastwood in his signature role as Dirty Harry, armed
with his signature Smith & Wesson Model 29, .44 caliber
SuperMag revolver, uttering his signature greeting to a
villainous criminal, "Go on, punk. Make my day!"

     It sounds harsh, but this is what the psalmist had in
mind for God to do to his enemies. The singer wanted to
make his enemies pay. Song 59 stops just shy of torture:
"But do not kill them, Lord, our shield, or people will
forget; By Thy strong power, bring them down, and make
them wander yet." He wanted to make them suffer.

     To imprecate is to call down curses and wrath on one's
enemy. This reminds us of the question Jesus' disciples

asked him in response to their not being welcomed into a Samaritan village, "Lord, do you want us to call down fire from heaven to destroy them? (Luke 9:54). But doesn't the New Testament categorically forbid this kind of behavior? "Do not take revenge, my dear friends, but leave room for God's wrath, for it is written: 'It is mine to avenge; I will repay,' says the Lord" (Rom. 12:19). It all depends on who is taking the revenge.

It all comes down to Calvin's dictum of a few days back, "It is God with whom we have to deal." Vengeance and wrath belong to God alone. I think the point (at least one of them) of the imprecatory psalms is actually to create a safe opportunity for the psalmist to get the gangster out of him- or herself. The only thing worse than having this kind of vengeful spirit is not finding a healthy way to expel it. It makes for the worst kind of sin sickness—equivalent to stage 4 small cell lung cancer.

Oh, there will be justice. It's just not mine to take. I must take the long view. I must take my inner gangster straight to the throne of God and sing out those dark melodies until they are no more. Yes, that's it. It's an offer we can't really afford to refuse.

So go ahead; make my day . . . sing this song.

Ask Yourself. Share with Another.

Is there anyone in your life you would like to call down fire on? How are you dealing with that? Where is God in the situation?

When You Are Ready to Throw in the Hotel-Room Towel

. . . .

PSALM 60

DUNDEE or ST. ANNE   86.86 C.M.
Words by Julie Tennent based on Psalm 60

1   O God, You have rejected us, and scattered us abroad;
    You have been very angry, but return to us, O God.

2   For You have made the earth to quake, and torn it
        open wide;
    Now heal its fractures, for it shakes and cannot
        long abide.

3   You've shown Your people desperate times, and
        hardship on them sent;
    And You have made us drink the wine of
        staggering lament.

4   And yet a banner You have giv'n to those who do
        fear You;
    That it may be displayed abroad, and witness to
        Your truth.

5 Save us and help with Your right hand; O hear and
      answer me;
   That those You love may come to be delivered and
      set free.

6 God spoke from His most holy place, "In triumph I
      will move;
   I'll parcel out both Shechem and the Valley
      of Succoth.

7 Now Gilead is mine by right; Manasseh mine shall be;
   Now Ephraim's my helmet; Judah's scepter is for me.

8 Moab's my washbowl; and my shoe on Edom I
      will throw;
   I'll shout over Philistia; in triumph I will go."

9 Who will bring me in strength up to the city fortified?
   And who will be the one that can to Edom lead
      and guide?

10 O God, is it not You who did reject and spurn us so?
    Will You not now return, O God—forth with our
       armies go?

11 O give us help against the foe, for help from man
       is vain;
12 Through God we'll gain the victory; He'll tread our
       foes again.

Consider This . . .

Some time ago, my family experienced the horrors of
moving for the second time in one year. Hyperbole?
Maybe. We relocated the first time from Kentucky to
Tennessee. The second move took us from the outskirts

of the city of Franklin to the heart of the community. Moving across town can be very deceptive. Something deep within tries to convince you that what took very large trucks to move you a few hundred miles will only take a few carloads to get across town. *Big mistake*. About halfway into the move, which took weeks instead of days because of this faulty approach, and after about the fifth night in the Embassy Suites, with seven of us crammed into one room, without clean socks, at the brink of civil war . . we needed Song 60.

> O God, You have rejected us, and scattered us
>   abroad;
> You have been very angry, but return to us, O God.

The details behind this psalm are somewhat complex, so here's the bottom line. King David found himself fighting battles on multiple fronts. While he was off fighting one battle, another enemy made a sneak attack on Jerusalem. And if that weren't enough, there was also an earthquake. The adage, "When it rains, it pours," comes to mind.

It's usually halfway into the job when things start to come unglued. You've come too far to turn back, but the obstacles seem too many to press on. It is in the mess of the middle that we must learn to sing the mixed melodies of hope and hopelessness. Song 60 shows the way.

Embracing uncertainty, we must sing both songs simultaneously. For example, today's song begins by lamenting the Lord's rejection, yet it ends with hopeful proclamation that "He'll tread our foes again."

It's never neat, and songs like these refuse to try and wrap it all up in a bow. These melodies leave lots of frayed loose ends. Something about singing out this angst of ambiguity to God has a way of moving us forward, even if we remain stuck in hotel-room hell for another week.

Give it a shot. Try on this melody for size.

Ask Yourself. Share with Another.

Does today's reading bring to mind any situation in your own life where hope is mingling with hopelessness? How about from your past? Think of others you know who are dealing with such contradictory confusion right now. Pray through Song 60 for them.

Sing it at soundtrack.seedbed.com

DAY 14

How the Great Songwriters Teach Us to Sing Life into the Face of Death

. . . .

PSALM 61

BEACH SPRING   87.87
Words by Julie Tennent based on Psalm 61

1   Hear my cry, O God my Savior, listen to my
         prayer below;
2   From the ends of earth I call You, as my heart grows
         faint and low.
     Lead me to the rock that's higher than I am, or e'er
         could go;
3   You have been my constant refuge, a strong tow'r
         against the foe.

4   How I long to dwell with You, God, in Your
         tent forevermore;
     And take refuge in the shelter of Your wings amidst
         the storm.
5   For You've heard the vows I've made, God, and You've
         given unto me
     the inheritance of all who fear Your name so faithfully.

6   Now increase the days the king lives; generations his
     years be.
7   May he be enthroned forever, in God's
     presence gloriously.
     Send Your love and faithful mercy to protect him all
     his days;
8   Then I will fulfill my vows and to Your name always
     sing praise.

Consider This . . .

I will forever remember the funeral of Martin Lee Walt, my grandfather. We knew the day was coming, and yet we all resisted it. Still, there we found ourselves, huddled as a family in the narthex of the church, a place so familiar to us, yet a place we had never known. The forced march down the long center aisle loomed before our grieving family. The patriarch of our clan lie in state, lifeless, at the front of the sanctuary. The Spirit beckoned us onward, down the well-worn path where so many had walked, crossing the ancient Rubicon of death itself.

All of a sudden, the doors to the great hall flew open, as though to reveal a bride entering the courts of her wedding. Then the organ started to play a song we knew so well in a way we had never heard it before. Five hundred years ago, writing under extreme duress, another Martin—Martin Luther—the battle-weary patron saint of the Great Reformation, penned a hymn for the ages, yet we heard it as though written for us, for this particular day in history: "A Mighty Fortress Is Our God."

A mighty fortress is our God, a bulwark never failing;
Our helper He, amid the flood of mortal ills prevailing:
For still our ancient foe doth seek to work us woe;
His craft and power are great, and, armed with cruel
    hate,
On earth is not his equal.

As we stepped into that small-town sanctuary,
the song surrounded us like a cosmic cathedral. The
cowering death march immediately transformed into a
parade of victory.

Did we in our own strength confide, our striving
    would be losing;
Were not the right Man on our side, the Man of God's
    own choosing:
Dost ask who that may be? Christ Jesus, it is He;
Lord Sabaoth, His name, from age to age the same,
And He must win the battle.

The ancient story of struggle, of life versus death, of
God versus Satan, rose up around us. Yes! He must win
the battle! Our collective vision lifted from the casket, the
emblem of death, to the cross towering above, the sign
that sang of ten thousand victories.

And though this world, with devils filled, should
    threaten to undo us,
We will not fear, for God hath willed His truth to
    triumph through us:
The Prince of Darkness grim, we tremble not for him;
His rage we can endure, for lo, his doom is sure,
One little word shall fell him.

One little word, a word that shouted the salvation of
all that is: "In the beginning was the Word, and the Word

was with God, and the Word was God" (John 1:1). This little word, the name of the Lord, rose up like a strong tower, and though by appearance we moved in a steady gait, in the Spirit we ran into that tower.

> That word above all earthly powers, no thanks to
>   them, abideth;
> The Spirit and the gifts are ours, through Him who
>   with us sideth:
> Let goods and kindred go, this mortal life also;
> The body they may kill: God's truth abideth still,
> His kingdom is forever.

We ran to the rock that was higher than ourselves. We raced into the tower of the name of the Lord. We stood in the fortress that is our mighty God. And for all the stony strength of these strong metaphors, the reality of it for us felt like being gathered under the wings of a protective parent, surrounded with the perfect peace of a holy love. It just doesn't get any better than this . . . until it does. And it will.

That's what Song 61 sings for me. It's a page out of the playbook of the songwriters of the ages.

If you are not ready to sing by now, you may want to check for a pulse . . .

Ask Yourself. Share with Another.

Do you know God as a refuge? Can you remember a time of challenge, struggle, or hardship where you ran to the Mighty Fortress?

DAY 15

The Penitential Psalms as a Counterinsurgency Field Manual

PSALM 38

MORNING SONG or DUNDEE   86.86 C.M.
Words by Julie Tennent based on Psalm 38

1   LORD, don't rebuke me in Your wrath, in anger don't
     chide me;
2   Your arrows pierce me and Your hand is heavy
     upon me.

3   Because of Your great wrath, I'm sick; my bones are
     weak from sin;
4   My guilt o'erwhelms me like a weight, too deep to
     bear within.

5   My wounds, they fester loathsomely, because of
     sinful pride;
6   I am bowed down, brought very low; and mourn all
     day inside.

7   My back is filled with searing pain; in me no health
     is found;

8   I'm feeble and crushed utterly; my anguished
        groans abound.

9   My longings lie before You, Lord; and You hear all
        my sighs;
10 With pounding heart, my strength fails me; the light's
        gone from my eyes.

11 My friends and neighbors stay away, because they see
        my lot;
12 Foes set their traps and seek my life, and all day long
        they plot.

13 I'm like the deaf who cannot hear; like mute, who
        cannot speak;
14 I'm like the one who does not hear, whose mouth no
        words can speak.

15 I wait for You, O Lord my God; and You will
        answer me;
16 For I said, "Do not let them gloat; exalt themselves
        o'er me."

17 For I am just about to fall; always my pain's within;
18 So I confess iniquity; I'm troubled by my sin.

19 Too many are my enemies, who hate me
        without cause;
20 They pay me evil for my good; and slander
        without pause.

21 O Lord, do not forsake me now, and be not far
        from me;
22 O Lord, my Savior, hear me now; come quickly to
        help me.

Consider This . . .

Do you remember those days in our recent national history when we thought the war in Iraq was over? President George W. Bush, dressed in fighter pilot garb, landed on the deck of the USS *Abraham Lincoln* aircraft carrier. After stepping out of the Navy S-3B fighter jet to great fanfare he gave a speech while standing in front of a massive banner, which read—you know what it read—"Mission Accomplished." In the sense that the sovereignty of Saddam Hussein's rule of Iraq had been defeated and temporarily transferred into the hands of the United States, yes, mission accomplished. No one seemed to realize the real war hadn't even started yet. The rule of Saddam had been cancelled, and yet this cancelled rule retained a form of rogue power and presence. It became known as the "insurgency." The United States, in cooperation with Iraqi police, began a war of a completely different order, known as the "counterinsurgency." General David Petraus wrote what is now famously known as the *Counterinsurgency Field Manual*.

When we place our faith in Jesus Christ as Savior, we are saved from the penalty of sin. In other words, any sin on the ledger of our lives—past, present, and future—is cancelled. The debt is paid in full by the atoning work of Jesus through his life, death, resurrection, and ascension to the right hand of God. The trouble with cancelled sin is that it retains a form of rogue power and presence. Recall a verse of Charles Wesley's most celebrated hymn, "O, For a Thousand Tongues to Sing":

> He breaks the power of canceled sin; He sets the
>   prisoner free.
> His blood can make the foulest clean, His blood
>   availed for me.

Are you seeing the analogy? Justification by grace through faith is mission accomplished, in the sense that the sovereignty of Satan's rule has been defeated and transferred into the hands of Jesus Christ. But the real war against the insurgency of sin is only getting started. What we need is a counterinsurgency field manual. And that's precisely what Song 38, and others like it, offer us.

The great reformer John Calvin once said of the Psalms that they are an anatomy of all parts of the soul. Today's psalm, Song 38, offers us one of the seven penitential psalms (6, 32, 38, 51, 102, 130, and 143). They are songs designed to help us repent and believe the gospel. The greatest impediment to our believing the gospel beyond mere assent to its truth is the sin believers continue to carry within them. The penitential psalms offer us a counterinsurgency field manual for the war against the insurgency of sin.

Ask Yourself. Share with Another.

Can you in any way identify with Song 38? Do you have any sense of the power of cancelled sin in your life? If not, you'd better be on the lookout for roadside bombs. Pray for the Holy Spirit to reveal the reality of your inner life, not for condemnation, but for the sake of deep change. Prepare yourself, though: it will awaken in you a holy discontent for more of God than you presently know. Trust that. Obey the promptings. It's the way that leads to Life.

And don't forget to sing.

DAY 16

There's Only One Way to Avoid Becoming What We Hate

PSALM 64

FOUNDATION or ST. DENIO   11.11.11.11
Words by Julie Tennent based on Psalm 64

1   O hear me, my God, as I cry unto You,
        Protect me from threats which the wicked will do.
2   O hide me when enemies seek to do wrong,
        And shelter me safe from the plots of the strong.

3   For they do all kinds of insidious things,
        They sharpen their tongues to unleash deadly stings.
4   They shoot from an ambush the innocent one,
        They shoot at him quickly, and fear have they none.

5   They bolster each other in their evil plans,
        They hide snares and say, "Who will know
           our commands?"
6   They plot great injustice; say, "We won't be found."
        The cunning of man's heart and mind knows
           no bound.

7   But God will shoot arrows at their hidden place,
     And they will be struck down, and found in disgrace.
8   Their own tongues will witness and make them forlorn,
     And all those who see them regard them with scorn.

9   All people will fear and together proclaim
     the works God has done, and they'll ponder His name.
10   Let all of the righteous rejoice in the LORD,
     Take refuge in Him, and to Him praise accord!

Consider This . . .

Something in me desperately wants to believe that people have gotten better over the centuries, that the human condition has somehow evolved or improved. If I am honest with myself, I must come to grips with the fact that as we were in the beginning, so are we now. Sin has grown only in its sophistication. Human beings are capable of unfettered wickedness and unimaginable cruelty. The murderous hatred of Cain. The deceptive cunning of Jacob. The vengeful wickedness of the brothers of Joseph. The duplicitous King David. And then there's Judas Iscariot. These bloodlines run deep in the human race.

Song 64 is a psalm of lament. In an age of positive thinking, laments can be unwelcome expressions of pessimism and dismissed as whining. To qualify as a lament, it must be framed in the larger context of hope. A lament is human sadness and longing lifted to God. Absent the presence of God and ultimate hope, we cannot lament; we can only despair. In the face of unresolved injustice, we lament before God. In the presence of unremitting enemy fire, we lament before God.

There's a hidden warning within the practice of lament. Singing lament is ultimately a protection from becoming infected with the situation we are lamenting. If we somehow skip God in the equation, taking it straight to the enemy, we will unwittingly and unknowingly become like our enemy. In this fashion, lament is not only protection from our enemy; it is salvation from becoming like our enemy.

Have the injustices you've endured and the enemies you have faced infected you with their hate-venom? As noted, the bloodline of Adam is inherently susceptible to this poison. In other words, we are all bearers of this blood type. The gospel is that God has introduced a new bloodline into the human race: the blood of his Son. It is the perfect and only antidote.

This forty-day study is leading us to the only place we can receive this lifeblood transfusion: the cross. Let us remember where the journey ends. In the face of his cruel tormenters (a.k.a. us) he takes his words straight to the courts of heaven, "Father, forgive them, for they do not know what they are doing" (Luke 23:34).

Do you realize that Jesus was singing a lament song from the cross? To follow him means singing along.

Ask Yourself. Share with Another.

Can you identify particular people in your life with whom you are very angry, even rising to the level of hate? Do you realize the toll this is taking on you? Are you ready to take a new approach? Would you consider taking it straight to God, in its raw, unadulterated form? He can handle it.

DAY 17

The Two Most Powerful
Words I've Ever Prayed

· ·

PSALM 74

PENITENTIA or MORECAMBE   10.10.10.10
Words by Julie Tennent based on Psalm 74

1   O God, why have You now rejected us?
    Why does Your anger burn against Your sheep?
2   You purchased us—Your own inheritance;
    Recall Your people, and Mount Zion keep.

3   Turn Your steps toward this devastation great;
    The en'my has destroyed the Holy Place.
4   Your foes have roared into Your meeting place,
    They've set up standards of their own disgrace.

5   They've taken axes as men would chop trees;
6   They've smashed the carved work,
    brought unholy shame;
7   They burned Your sanctuary to the ground;
    Defiled the dwelling place of Your great name.

8   They said within their hearts, "We'll crush
      them whole!"
    They burned each place where worship was of Thee;

63

9   No mighty signs or prophets can be found,
     And none of us knows how long this will be.

10   How long, O God, will foes deride Your name?
     How long will enemies their scorn deploy?
11   Why do You hold Your hand back and delay?
     Take Your right hand from waiting, and destroy!

12   You, O my God, are my king from of old;
     You bring salvation upon the earth;
13   You split the seas wide open by Your pow'r.
14   You crushed the monsters and Leviathan's girth.

15   You opened springs and dried up rivers' flow;
16   The day and night, sun, moon belong to You;
17   You set earth's bound'ries; where they end, You know;
     You made the summer and the winter, too.

18   Now, Lᴏʀᴅ, remember how Your foes do mock,
     How foolish people have reviled Your name;
19   Don't hand Your dove to wild beasts to devour,
     And don't forget Your people, clothed in shame.

20   Keep Your own covenant, O Lord, in mind,
     For dark and violence now fill all the land;
21   Don't let Your poor, oppressed, no mercy find,
     But may the needy praise Your mighty hand.

22   Rise up, O God, and now defend Your cause;
     See how fools mock You each day scornfully;
23   Do not ignore the clamor of Your foes;
     Their uproar rises up continually.

Consider This . . .

Song 74 reminds me of a time several years ago when we
hosted my friend Pete Greig, the leader of an international

prayer movement, for the opening of the Asbury House of Prayer. At the close of one of his evening messages, after recounting the devastating need for God amid the ruins of the world, he led the packed house in an unbelievably simple yet unforgettably powerful prayer. He instructed us that all five hundred of us were going to pray aloud at the same time, as loudly as we possibly could, for a duration of five minutes. The prayer would consist of two words: "Come On!"

Never before and never since have I been part of such a powerful crying out to God. Just two words. Talk about "storming the gates"! I'm not sure I had ever shouted like that before in my life. Take the most raucous athletic contest you've ever attended and multiply that by three and you will get close. Though it took a moment to gain the self-permission to do such a thing, the praying soon took on the quality of abandoned impatience, of a deeply desperate emotional pleading. "Come On! Come On! Come On! Come On!"

The singer makes an interesting play with Song 74. Most laments tend to center around the woes of those who are lamenting. The words of the prayers focus around their own pain and despair. Song 74 takes another tack. After likely exhausting the depths of the pain of the people, the poet drills down into the angst of the Almighty. The shame is no longer located with the people. It now lands squarely on God. Note how many times we see the words "You" and "Your" and "Thee."

It is as though the singer stands before God and says things like, "How long are you going to take this? They are making a mockery of you! How long are you going to take this? They are making you look weak! Come on, Yahweh! Not only have they burned your house, but they are systematically erasing your memory from your land! Come on!" Then the song reminds God of his own glorious record in a play-by-play kind of way. The singer appeals boldly to God to arise and defend his own honor, for his own sake.

So as you read today's paper or watch the evening news; as you see the unbearable suffering in a place like war-torn Syria and countless others, think about Song 74 and remember the two little words. And if you are feeling bold, go for it. "Come On! Come On! Come On! Come On!"

Before you get to the shout, you may want to try the song. Sing Song 74 now.

Ask Yourself. Share with Another.

Can you think of a situation in your life in which you want to scream out, "Come on!" to God? Try finding a place where no one can hear you and go for it.

Sing it at soundtrack.seedbed.com

DAY 18

How to Pray When the Lights Are On but Nobody's Home

. . . .

PSALM 77

KINGSFOLD, ST. ANNE, or DUNDEE   86.86 C.M.
Words by Julie Tennent based on Psalm 77

1   I cried out to my God for help; I cried for God to hear;
2   When in distress, I sought the Lord, no comfort was
      found near.

    All night I stretched untiring hands; my soul could
      only moan;
3   I mused, my spirit grew more faint; remembered God
      with groans.

4   You kept my eyes from closing, Lord, too troubled
      e'en to speak;
5   I thought of days from long ago, when faith did not
      seem weak.

6   My songs remembered in the night bring mem'ry to
      my heart;
    My spirit does inquire of God; with musing,
      questions start:

7   "Will God reject forever? O where has His favor gone?
8   Has His unfailing love now failed? His promise
        trusted long?   ˙

9   Has God forgotten to be kind and merciful to me?
    Has He in anger withheld love? No mercy do I see!"

10 And then I thought, "It is my grief and my infirmity;
    I will appeal to God's right hand—the years that I
        can see."

11 I will remember the Lord's deeds, Your miracles of old;
12 I'll meditate on all Your works, Your mighty deeds
        once told.

13 Your ways, O God, are holy, and no god's great as
        our God.
14 The God who performs miracles, displays Your
        pow'r abroad.

15 Your mighty arm redeemed the host of people
        who descend
    from Jacob and from Joseph—You great help to them
        did send.

16 The waters saw You and they shook; the waters saw
        with fear;
    The very depths were shaken when Your presence,
        God, drew near.

17 The clouds outpoured their water, and the skies with
        thunder shook;
    Your lightning arrows flashed about; all trembled at
        Your look.

18 Your thunder in the whirlwind roared, and all who
        heard did shake;
    Your lightning lit the world, and all the earth did fear
        and quake.

19 Your path led through the mighty sea; Your way
       through waters deep;
    And though Your footprints were not seen, Your
       people you did keep.

20 You led Your people like a flock which trusts the
       shepherd's hand;
    Through Moses and through Aaron, You enabled them
       to stand.

Consider This . . .

Yesterday in my reflection, I mentioned Pete Greig, one of the founders of a worldwide prayer movement. If you want to read a page-turner treatment of that story, take a look at *Red Moon Rising: How 24-7 Prayer Is Awakening a Generation*. More surprising, though, is the title of Greig's next book, *God on Mute: Engaging the Silence of Unanswered Prayer*. Song 77 is all about that second title.

   Jesus was clear about this. Remember when he told the story about trying to wake someone up late at night to get some food to help another friend in need? The man responded to the knocking with this helpful reply: "Don't bother me. The door is already locked, and my children and I are in bed. I can't get up and give you anything" (Luke 11:7). The point of the story was to create a comparison and a contrast. First for the comparison: at times it's going to feel as though your prayers are bouncing off the ceiling, that the lights are on but nobody's home, or at least they don't want to get out of bed. The contrast: God is nothing like the guy who doesn't want to get out of bed.

The big point: never stop asking, seeking, and knocking. Do not despair. God is working.

Song 77 makes a decisive turn with this line:

> And then I thought, "It is my grief and my infirmity;
> I will appeal to God's right hand—the years that I can
>   see."

It's as if he reasoned with himself that all this despair about being forgotten and rejected by God was not really about God, but his own grief and infirmity. Far from a "double-down on the effort because I don't have enough faith" approach, the singer begins to ask, seek, and knock with a new tactic: memory. The lyrics to the song make a beeline straight to the Red Sea. But note: the psalmist pitches his tent on the far side of the sea. Pure brilliance.

> Your path led through the mighty sea; Your way
>   through waters deep;
> And though Your footprints were not seen, Your
>   people You did keep.

The best predictor of future performance is past performance. Though the old adage is often not true with people, it's always true with God. Yesterday. Today. Forever. Never give up. There's a campsite still here with plenty of room for you to pitch your tent for a while.

Ask Yourself. Share with Another.

Are you feeling as if God is on mute, when it comes to your prayers of late? Try to remember a past story or sign of the faithfulness of God in your life. Now try singing this song.

DAY 19

You Don't Have to Be a Singer to Sing

PSALM 4

DUKE STREET, ROCKINGHAM OLD, or SWEET HOUR   88.88 L.M. D
Words by Timothy Tennent based on Psalm 4

1   God, answer when I call to You,
    For You are all my righteousness;
    Be merciful, and hear my prayer,
    O give me hope in my distress.

2   People of earth, how long will you
    my glory turn into disgrace?
    How long will you love worthless lies,
    And seek false gods and not my face?

3   The LORD has placed us with Himself
    and hears us when we call to Him.
4   So in your anger, do not sin;
    And search your heart as day grows dim.

    O ponder Him upon your bed;
    Be still, and make your heart His own;
5   Give sacrifices which are right;
    Trust in the LORD, the Lord alone.

6   So many ask, "O who can know
     or show us any good at all?"
     O let the light of Your face shine
     upon us, Lord, who on You call.

7   My heart is filled with greater joy
     than when new wine and grain abound;
8   I will lie down and sleep in peace;
     For You, Lord, safely me surround.

Consider This . . .

Do you sing?

Have you bought or downloaded a record or a song lately and headed straight for the liner notes to read the lyrics with no interest in actually hearing it sung or singing along? Who would do that? Imagine it: buying a record, pulling out the liner notes, and throwing the CD away.

But is this not what we do with the Psalms?

Something about singing takes words beyond our rational faculties and into the heart of our emotional realities. This is why there is a songbook in the middle of the Bible. Singing is the *sine qua non* of life. It means "essential." The life hidden with Christ in God is a singing life. Why? Because this life is much more about the proper ordering of our desires, affections, dispositions, and deepest feelings than about managing behavior and measuring performance.

So do you sing?

Remember the words of Nicetas, "For a psalm is sweet to the ear when sung, it penetrates the soul when it gives pleasure, it is easily remembered when sung often, and what the harshness of the Law cannot force from the minds of man it excludes by the suavity of song."[4]

Don't tell me you are not a singer. I'm not asking if you are a singer. I want to know if you sing. Maybe this is the problem: we think that in order to sing, we must be singers. In this American Idol culture, has singing become more about performance than pathos? Sure, there's always emotion in song, and we experience it when we listen, but that's not enough. To sing is to move beyond experience and into expression. This is what the Psalms are for.

I have been careful through these daily Lenten writings to label them as songs for a reason. What if we stopped saying the word "psalms" for a while and referred to these 150 chapters of the Bible as "the Songs"? Instead of saying the Twenty-third Psalm, we could say the Twenty-third Song. Song 23.

One more time. Do you sing? It's a serious question.

Psalm 4 is a short, easy one to sing.

Ask Yourself. Share with Another.

So are you giving singing these songs a shot? Why not? You won't know until you try.

How Scripture Is Like a Software Agreement . . . Until It's Not

. . . .

PSALM 5

REDHEAD or DIX   77.77.77
Words by Timothy Tennent based on Psalm 5

1   Give ear to my words, O LORD,
    My deep groaning don't ignore.
2   Hear and heed my pleading prayer,
    As I come and seek Your care.
    King and God, to You I pray,
    I will watch for You this day.

3   In the morning, hear my voice.
    In the morning, I'll rejoice;
    Bring my prayers before Your throne,
    Wait in hope for You alone.
4   You love not the wrong we do;
    Evil cannot dwell with You.

5   Pride can't stand before Your eyes,
    Those who do wrong You despise.
6   You destroy those who tell lies,
    Men of bloodshed You chastise;

7   But by mercy I will come;
     Humbly bow within Your home.

8   Lead me in Your righteousness,
     For my foes cause me distress;
     Make Your way straight before me,
9   For their words can't trusted be;
     Their throat is an open grave,
     Heart is dark, and tongue can't save.

10   Make them bear their guilt, O God,
     Let them fall by their own fraud.
     Banish them for all their sin,
     For they have rebelled within;
     By their own intrigues they fall,
     Hold them guilty, God of all.

11   But those who do hide in You,
     Let them ever sing anew.
     Spread protection over them,
     That they may rejoice again;
12   For You bless the righteous, Lord,
     Keep them by Your shield and sword.

Consider This . . .

One of the unwitting ways I have tended to approach the Psalms (and the whole Bible, for that matter) is the same way I approach software agreements. I click the little box following the word *accept*. I read through a psalm like the one from today, and I accept it and move on. I assent to its truth and move on.

The problem with this? Scripture is not asking for our acceptance. It is not requesting that we assent to its truth. Scripture, the Word of God, requires our embodied engagement. The Word of God is always looking to land itself in human flesh, not just in the ephemerality of one's passing thoughts. Reading it aloud is a step in the right direction.

Ask Yourself. Share with Another.

Ever try singing a software agreement? It just doesn't work that way. Is anything holding you back from singing?

Why Singing the Psalms Is a Matter of Life and Death

. . . .

PSALM 70

SOUTHWELL or ST. THOMAS   66.86 S.M.
Words by Julie Tennent based on Psalm 70

1   O God, deliver me; O Lᴏʀᴅ, make haste—help me!
2   Let those ashamed and humbled be who seek my
        life wrongly.

     May all who seek my end, who in my hurt delight;
     Be turned back in disgrace, O Lord; dishonored in
        Your sight.

3   May all who say to me, "Aha, Aha!" in spite;
     May they be turned back in their shame; hear me, O
        God of might.

4   But may all who seek You; be glad, with joy abide;
     May those who love salvation say, "Let God
        be magnified!"

5   Still I'm afflicted, Lord; make haste, O God, I pray;
     You're my deliverer and help; O Lᴏʀᴅ, do not delay!

Consider This . . .

Over the years I have made many trips to the Abbey of Gethsemani for days of spiritual warfare. I always join the monks as they sing the Songs (Psalms). I learn from them what it looks like to put on the full armor of God. Every two weeks they systematically sing through all 150 Psalms, gathering seven times a day, seven days a week. Every single time, they begin their singing prayers with the opening lines of Song 70. I can hear their chant now as they sing these words: "O God, come to my assistance; O Lord, make haste to help me" (DV).

Have you ever considered that the Psalms are Scripture's strongest strategy of spiritual warfare? These songs train us for the unconventional warfare of the Holy Spirit. In singing them, we heed Paul's exhortation to the Ephesians: "Finally, be strong in the Lord and in his mighty power. Put on the full armor of God, so that you can take your stand against the devil's schemes" (Eph. 6:10–11).

The chief scheme of the devil is to convince us that our enemy is other people and lure us into an offensive attack. To be sure, our enemy does come in the form of other people. Because these enemies have become the unwitting and unknowing pawns of darkness, we must learn to pray, "Father, forgive them, for they know not what they do" (Luke 23:34 ESV). Paul reminds us, "For our struggle is not against flesh and blood, but against the rulers, against the authorities, against the powers of this dark world and against the spiritual forces of evil in the heavenly realms" (Eph. 6:12).

God is not looking for people to fight for him. Remember his word to Moses on the Egyptian shore of the Red Sea, "Do not be afraid. Stand firm and you will see the deliverance the LORD will bring you today. The Egyptians you see today you will never see again" (Exod. 14:13). The warfare of the Spirit teaches us to stand firm. (Four times we see this call to "stand" in the span of five verses.)

"Therefore put on the full armor of God, so that when the day of evil comes, you may be able to stand your ground, and after you have done everything, to stand" (Eph. 6:13).

And what is this armor? Truth. Righteousness. Peace. Faith. Salvation. The Word of the Lord. It is primarily in singing these songs of deliverance that we put on this invisible yet impenetrable armor.

Perhaps the most pressing lesson of these Songs comes from the words of the one who wrote so many of them. Facing an opponent twice his size, against all odds, David, without armor, shield, or sword, spoke to the giant Goliath, "The battle belongs to the LORD!" (See 1 Samuel 17.)

I repeat, spiritual warfare is not fighting with some kind of jihadist ethic against Satan. It is about standing firm in the full armor of God. Singing these songs makes us strong in the Lord and in his mighty power. Are you getting this?

There is an absolute urgency to singing these songs. It's not a "nice" devotional exercise. It's a matter of life and death.

Ask Yourself. Share with Another.

Have you considered the Songs as tactics of spiritual warfare? Will you?

DAY 22

The Journey from "Born this Way" to "Born Again"

PSALM 51

DUNDEE, NEW BRITAIN, CRIMOND, or SALZBURG   86.86 C.M.
Words by Timothy and Julie Tennent based on Psalm 51

1   From Your unfailing love, O God,
      Have mercy upon me;
      Blot out transgressions, cleanse from sin,
2   Purge my iniquity.

3   For my transgressions and my sin
      are always in Your sight;
4   'Gainst You alone, I've evil done,
      And turned from what is right.

      So You are right when You do speak
      and judge me from within;
5   For from the time I was conceived,
      I have been trapped in sin.

6   For truth is what You call us to,
      Formed in our inward parts;
      You teach me wisdom day by day,
      In the depths of my heart.

7   Cleanse me with hyssop, make me clean;
     Wash me—I'll be as snow;
8   Let me hear joy, let bones rejoice
     which You once crushed below.

9   O hide Your face from all my sins,
     Blot out iniquity;
10   Create in me a pure heart, God;
     Renew Your life in me.

     Renew my steadfast spirit, God,
11   And cast me not from You;
     Don't take Your Holy Spirit, Lord,
     From me; Your Spirit true.

12   Restore to me salvation's joy,
     And grant, O Lord, to me
     a spirit willing to praise You
     and then sustained I'll be.

13   Then I'll teach sinners of Your ways
     and they will turn to You;
14   Save me from bloodguilt, Savior God;
     My tongue will sing Your truth.

15   Lord, open up my lips, my mouth
     will Your great praise declare;
16   You don't delight in sacrifice,
     Or I would bring it there.

17   The sacrifices You require
     are broken, contrite hearts;
     O God, You won't despise these if
     they're from our inward parts.

18   With pleasure, prosper Zion, Lord,
     Build up Jerusalem;

19   Then righteous off'rings will be made;
      And You'll delight in them.

Consider This . . .

Can you remember your first real sin? I remember mine. I stole twenty dollars from my mother's wallet, and to make it okay, I went out into the backyard, wadded up the money, threw it on the ground, and walked away about ten yards. Then I turned back around and walked back over to—surprisingly and delightfully—find a twenty-dollar bill wadded up on the ground. Someone must have dropped it! Brilliant! Then I invoked the "finders keepers" rule. Next I made the ill-fated decision to run and tell my mom of my good fortune. How long do you think it took her to do the math on that one? Exactly.

That's the junior version of stealing someone else's wife, getting her pregnant, and then arranging her husband's death. In case you aren't aware, Song 51 was David's confession in response to his treacherous sin.

I used to think I became a real sinner on that ill-fated day in the backyard. Now I know better. I used to think I was a sinner because I sinned. This song tells me the hard truth. I was born this way. I was born into the corrupted lineage of the human race. I am not a sinner because I sin. I sin because I am a sinner. Major difference!

There's a bigger question afoot here. Am I destined to always sin? Am I forever stuck in the broken category of "sinner"? Can this cancer be cured, or is managing the size of the tumor the best we can hope for? If I was born this way, what are the implications of being born again?

Though a far, far cry from it today, the Methodist movement believed in and experienced a cure. They used the old-fashioned biblical term for it: *sanctification*. They believed a person could become so infused with the holiness of the love of God that sin would actually lose its hold on him. Another way of saying this is these men and women took the gospel at its word.

In a letter he wrote to a Mr. Walter Churchey, John Wesley put into words what he saw happening:

> Entire sanctification, or Christian perfection, is neither more nor less than pure love; love expelling sin, and governing both the heart and life of a child of God. The refiner's fire purges out all that is contrary to love, and that many times by a pleasing smart. Leave all this to Him that does all things well, and that loves you better than you do yourself.[5]

Do you believe this is possible? Your answer will be determinative of your future.

Song 51 is the beginning of the cure.

Ask Yourself. Share with Another.

Do you believe it is possible to grow so full of the love of God that sin as you know it loses its power over you? Why or why not?

DAY 23

The Secret to Getting Past Insecurity

PSALM 142

REDHEAD or DIX   77.77.77
Words by Julie Tennent based on Psalm 142

1   I cry to the LORD Most High,
     Lift my voice with plaintive cry;
2   Pour out my complaint to Him,
     Tell the trouble I am in.
     Lord, in mercy think on me,
     Hear my supplicating plea.

3   When my spirit does grow faint,
     I trust You hear my complaint.
     You it is who know my way;
     Know the path I walk each day.
     Foes have hid a snare for me,
     Hid a trap I cannot see.

4   Look to my right hand and see,
     No one is concerned for me.
     I've no refuge—none who care;
5   I cry, "LORD, You must be there!

You're my refuge, my portion,
In the land of living ones."

6   Listen to my cry and heed,
     For I am in desperate need.
     Save me from those who pursue,
     They are not too strong for You.
     Rescue me and hear my plea,
     For they are too strong for me.

7   Set me from my prison free,
     That my praise to You might be.
     Righteous ones will gather round
     to hear how You did confound;
     They will all Your goodness see
     how You loved me bountifully.

Consider This . . .

I have a major problem. I knew it from a young age. I've fought it all my life, and the more I try to overcome it, the worse it gets. I can bring this condition down to one word. You're probably thinking, he's going to talk about sin again, and "being born this way," and all the other stuff he says over and over and over again. That would be predictable, but that's not my problem. Okay. It *is* my problem, but that's not the problem I'm talking about today. Actually, I think this is the problem that underlies the problem of sin.

I'm just going to say it: I am insecure. I felt it from a young age—that inner gnawing just under the surface of things, that almost constantly messages you that things are not okay, that you don't cut it, that you just don't have what it takes. Did you catch the slick move I made in that last sentence? I slipped out of talking about *my* problem and began to make it *your* problem. That move from speaking in first person to second person gets me every time. It's as if I'm saying, "No, I know you have this problem too, and I would much rather analyze your problem than deal with my own."

So as a safe play for both of us, let's just shift this to the third person, who in this instance happens to be the psalmist. Can you believe how insecure the psalmist is? We are at Song 142, for crying out loud—only eight more left in the songbook—and he is still talking about his desperation and neediness and sad circumstance. "Own your life! Make a plan, bro," I want to tell him. "Hire a security guard already!"

In truth, the singer shows us the only real way to deal with the problem of insecurity. The secret to getting past insecurity is to let it lead you to vulnerability before God. Song 142 is a great example. The singer teaches us the only security to be had is the intimate presence of Almighty God.

Jesus made it the first attitude in his "8 Attitudes of Highly Successful Insecure People," otherwise known as The Beatitudes: "Blessed are the poor in spirit, for theirs is the kingdom of heaven" (Matt. 5:3). Somewhere along the way of my growing up, I came across this translation of this verse: "Blessed are those who know their need of God . . ." My working translation today is, "Blessed are the insecure, for the security of heaven is theirs."

If we will go there, these 150 Songs will lead us to the rock that is higher than us, to the only secure place on the planet—the kingdom of God.

It's kind of like an Alcoholics Anonymous for the rest of us: "I'm John David, and I'm insecure, and I'm discovering day by day the only security on the planet that brings me true happiness. His name is Jesus."

Will you join me in singing Song 142?

Ask Yourself. Share with Another.

Are you in touch with your own insecurity? What keeps you from admitting it? Or are you finding true security in a relationship with Jesus Christ?

Sing it at soundtrack.seedbed.com

DAY 24

Could It Really Be That Simple?

PSALM 40

NEW BRITAIN, CRIMOND, SALZBURG, MORNING SONG,
or DUNDEE   86.86 C.M.
Words by Julie Tennent based on Psalm 40

1   I waited for the LORD my God; I waited patiently,
    And He in mercy heard my cry; inclined His ear to me.
2   He brought me up out of the pit, out from the
        miry clay;
    He set my feet upon a rock, there firm to stand
        and stay.

3   He put a new song in my mouth, God's praise for all
        to hear;
    And many then will trust the LORD, who see and learn
        to fear.
4   How blest the one who trusts the LORD, who looks not
        to the proud,
    Nor to the ones who turn aside to false gods
        all around.

5   For many are Your wonders, LORD, things planned
        beyond compare;

> They are more than I can recount, more than I
> could declare.

6 An off'ring You have not required, but rather pierced
my ears;
Burnt off'ring You have not desired, but rather, one
who hears.

7 And so I said, "Behold, I come; it is prescribed for me
8 within Your scroll to do Your will; Your law is deep
in me."
9 I have proclaimed deliverance; glad news for all
to hear;
You know I've not restrained my lips from speaking far
and near.

10 I do not hide Your righteousness alone within
my heart,
But I speak of Your faithfulness; Your truth I do impart.
I've not concealed Your steadfast love, Your
faithfulness of old;
To the assembly gathered round, I've Your
salvation told.

11 Do not withhold Your mercy, Lord, or keep it far
from me,
May Your great love and faithfulness keep
me continually.
12 For troubles have surrounded me, iniquities flood me;
More than the hairs upon my head, my heart fails
within me.

13 Be pleased, O Lord, to save me; and come quickly to
my aid;
For many seek to take my life; let them now
be dismayed.

14 Let those be turned back, put to shame, who in my
       harm delight,
    Leave them appalled and desolate who would destroy
       my life.

15 Let those who say to me, "Aha!" be appalled at
       their shame;
16 But may all who seek You rejoice and be glad in
       Your name.
    May those who love salvation say, "Exalt the
       LORD always!"
17 Yet I am needy; think of me! My God, do not delay!

Consider This . . .

"I waited patiently."
    He did everything else.
    Time to sing.

Ask Yourself. Share with Another.

Can you identify a place or places where you find yourself waiting on the Lord? Does waiting patiently have to
mean waiting passively? What might active, yet patient,
waiting look like?

DAY 25

Why No One Laments on *The Walking Dead*

- -

PSALM 79

PASSION CHORALE   76.76
Words by Julie Tennent based on Psalm 79

1   The nations have invaded Your heritage, O God;
     They have defiled Your temple; Jerus'lem's now
       but sod.

2   They've given the dead bodies of Your own saints
       as meat,
     As food to birds of heaven, and beasts of earth
       to eat.

3   They've poured out blood like water
       around Jerusalem;
     The dead are strewn, there's no one to care or
       bury them.

4   We're objects of reproach to our
       neighbors everywhere,
     Of scoffing and derision to those around us there.

5   How long, O Lord? Forever will You be filled with ire?
     How long will jealousy and Your anger burn like fire?

6   Pour out Your wrath on nations who don't respect
         Your fame;
      Your anger on the kingdoms that don't call on
         Your name.

7   For they've devoured Jacob, his homeland laid
         to waste;
8   Don't hold the sins of fathers against us—come
         in haste!
9   Help us, O God our Savior! For glory of Your name;
      Deliver and forgive us, for the sake of Your name.

10   Why should the nations, boasting, in pride say,
         "Where's their God?"
      Before our eyes, make known to the nations
         far abroad,
      That You avenge Your people and see their
         blood outpoured,
      That You, before our eyes, show Yourself to be
         the Lord.

11   May groaning of the pris'ners come to Your ear
         and eye;
      By greatness of Your power, preserve those doomed
         to die.
12   Pay back into the laps of our neighbors sevenfold
      reproach that they have hurled, Lord; and insults they
         have told.

13   Then we who are Your people—the sheep of Your
         own field—
      will thank You, and forever all praise to You we'll yield.
      And from one generation unto all length of days,
      We will recount Your glory, and will tell forth
         Your praise.

Consider This . . .

Post-apocalyptic literature is on the rise these days. From movies like *The Road* and *World War Z* to the popular AMC series *The Walking Dead*, the post-apocalyptic genre is all about the meaninglessness of a life without hope. In these stories, conditions are so far beyond bad that concepts like justice and even civilization are beyond imagining. There's not much singing going on.

That's what is surprising about Song 79. It has all the tones and strains of post-apocalyptic storytelling. The people of God had endured cataclysmic tragedy. Take a second look at those first two stanzas. It's worse than bad. The big difference between this song and others like it? There is a bigger story surrounding the apocalypse. This bigger story creates the reality of hope. And hope creates the possibility for genuine lament.

What is missing in today's post-apocalyptic stories is hope, and consequently they are devoid of lament. Life has been reduced to mere survival. There is no bigger story. Sure, there's plenty of personal drama, but no one is crying out to God in any significant way.

I'm coming to the conclusion that lament is the authenticating sign of hope, and consequently a key indicator of real faith in God.

And remember, lament is a song.

Ask Yourself. Share with Another.

Have you resigned yourself to some inevitable, unfavorable outcome concerning a situation in your life? In other words, have you let go of hope? Are you just trudging on? Surviving? Would you be willing to take the risk to lament over this situation before God? Can you wrap your mind around a story bigger than the one defeating you right now?

DAY 26

Are You a Thinker or a Feeler? When Head and Heart Connect

PSALM 28

KINGSFOLD, DUNDEE, or ST. ANNE   86.86 C.M.
Words by Julie Tennent based on Psalm 28

1   To You I call, O LORD my Rock; don't turn Your ear
    from me,
    For if You're silent, then like those within the pit I'll be.
2   O, hear my cry for mercy, as to You for help I call;
    As I lift up my hands to the Most Holy Place of all.

3   With wicked who much evil do, do not drag me away;
    Who speak peace with their friends, while hate is in
    their hearts all day.
4   Repay them for their evil work, for deeds their hands
    have done;
    Bring back on them what they deserve, the evil of
    each one.

5   Since they do not regard the LORD, nor works His
    hands have done;
    He'll tear them down, and never build back up a
    single one.

6   Praise to the Lord, for He has heard my cry for grace
     from Him;
7   The Lord's my strength and shield; I'm helped as my
     heart trusts in Him.

     My heart does leap for joy, and I give thanks to Him
     in song;
8   The Lord's His people's strength, a fortress of
     salvation strong.
9   O save Your people, and do bless Your
     own inheritance;
     And be their shepherd, carry them—forever
     their defense.

Consider This . . .

I live in my head most of the time. I am far more rational
than I am emotional. In fact, I have trained myself to take
whatever emotion I might be feeling and quickly move
it into the chamber of my thoughts, where I can think
about it and be more in control. It might be said of me
that I live from my head. Many others are just the oppo-
site. They are governed by their emotions. Their capacity
to feel often overrides any analytical frameworks.

In the present age, we have come to think about
people as either feelers or thinkers. We speak in terms of
the dual realities of the head and the heart as though they
were two separate places. As a result, we tend to wind up
with either an overactive intellect or an overwhelming
intuition. Both of these scenarios result from becoming
trapped and isolated in our inner world. We live in our
heads or in our hearts.

This taxonomy is foreign to the psalmist. Why? Because the psalmist sees these as one integrated reality. There is no head and heart. There is the situation, the person (or the people), and God. The psalmist has learned to live in the situation, out loud, in the holy mingling of feeling and thought, before God. There is no escaping into thoughts on the one hand or feelings on the other. The interior life integrates itself openly and outwardly in the safety of the sanctuary of presence of God. Whatever is inside, the psalmist sings out unto God. The psalmist trains us to live deeply from our innermost self, yet in an open, honest, unveiled, and out loud way before God. I want you to take a look at Ephesians 3:14–19 and see if this is not exactly what Paul was praying for us to experience.

This is why music and singing and song are so essential to being a human. Song leads us into a place where *knowing* gets beyond intellect and *feeling* gets beyond emotion. Singing leads to an "outing" of our inner person. We speak often about head and heart connecting at the point of our hands, which does have a nice alliterative ring to it, but I believe that head and heart (whatever those actually are) come together in our audible voices, when we sing it all out before God.

Ask Yourself. Share with Another.

What do you think? How do you feel about this? What's holding you back? Others hearing you? Could this be why Jesus said to go into a room, close the door, and go for it?

DAY 27

On Learning to Pray: From Polite Conversation to Crying Out to God

PSALM 56

ST. ANNE, DUNDEE, or MORNING SONG   86.86 C.M.
Words by Julie Tennent based on Psalm 56

1   Be merciful to me, O God, for vile men pursue me;
All through the day they come at me, strongly
      attacking me.

2   They slander me as they pursue, all day they've
      cruelly lied;
How many are attacking me with arrogance
      and pride.

3   When I'm afraid, I'll trust in You, in God whose word
      I praise;
4   In God I trust; I will not fear; what harm can mere
      men raise?

5   But all day long they twist my words, they plot to
      bring me strife;
6   They lurk and watch my steps, conspire to take away
      my life.

7   On no account let them escape, in anger bring
       them down.
8   Keep my tears in Your scroll, O God; let my
       lament resound.

9   Then all my foes will be turned back, when for Your
       help I call;
     By this I'll know that You're with me, and will not let
       me fall.

10   In God, whose word I praise, I'll trust—
       in Yahweh faithfully;
11   In God I trust, I will not fear; what can man do to me?

12   I'm under vows to You, O God; I will present to You
       the offerings that give You thanks—to my vows I'll
       be true.

13   For You delivered me from death, my feet from
       stumbling strife;
     That I may walk before You, God, within the light
       of life.

Consider This . . .

By the time we get to Song 56, life stinks for David. The
anointed king of Israel finds himself far from the throne
and on the run from the rogue royal, Saul. The giant-
slayer seeks refuge in the giant's home country. How
could things go so wrong for one who held so much
promise?

We don't too often find ourselves with such violent
enemies as David did, but we know what it's like for our
best-laid plans to go south. Whether you are dealing with

murderous threats or you got passed over for the promotion, one of the biggest lessons of the Psalms is also the most obvious one: cry out to God! By now, we know the Psalms are not sanitized prayers for the suburbs. They are the gut-wrenching cries of real people who need immediate help.

I remember the years when my life, as I'd planned it, began to disintegrate. Armed with a résumé to kill for, heading into my second year of law school, at the peak of privilege, I basked in a sea of opportunities. On the eve of writing my golden ticket, I awakened to a knowing beyond knowledge that I was headed down the wrong path for my life. Another calling arrested me, and I resisted as if it were the plague. In those days, for the first time, I learned to cry out to God. Literally. This went on for months. Though what I cried out for did not happen (a release from this calling), absolutely everything else did change. I'm not sure what I considered prayer to be before those days, but in light of my crying out to God, it was polite conversation and unholy small talk.

It's a longer story I will save for later, but suffice it to say, I have never been the same since.

Start thinking of the Psalms as a school of prayer.

Ask Yourself. Share with Another.

Have you discovered a place of prayer beyond polite petitions? Would you be willing to go into a room, close the door, and voice aloud your situation before God? Even though he knows it, speak out your situation before God.

This is the only way it gets out of your own anxious spirit and into God's hands. Don't underestimate the importance of this simple step. It's not just a good idea; it's an essential practice.

The Odds Are Never in Our Favor, or, Why Optimism Isn't the Solution for Pessimism

· ·

PSALM 140

BEACH SPRING or STUTTGART   87.87
Words by Julie Tennent based on Psalm 140

1 Rescue me, O LORD, from evil, violent men—
   O protect me!
2 They devise plans in their hearts and stir up
   evil constantly.

3 They make tongues as sharp as serpents, poison is
   upon their lips;
4 Keep me, LORD, protect me from them, for my feet
   they plan to trip.

5 Proud men hide a snare to catch me, they set traps
   along my way.
6 I cry, "LORD, You are my God"; and for Your mercy I
   will pray.

7   Sovereign LORD, my strong deliverer; for the fight,
        Your shield I need;
8   Don't grant wicked their desires, LORD; do not let their
        plans succeed.

9   May all those who do surround me be entrapped in
        their own lies;
10   Burning coals fall down upon them, thrown in fire,
        never to rise.

11   Let not slander be established; anywhere the
        land around;
     Those who slander, men of violence—may disaster
        hunt them down.

12   For I know the LORD loves justice, and upholds the
        needy's cause;
13   And the upright ones will praise You; they will live
        who love Your laws.

Consider This . . .

Because of my brutal realism at times, people often mistake me for a pessimist. Early in our friendship, in response to my grim assessment of a particular situation, my friend asked me in a slightly sarcastic tone, "So J. D., are you a pessimist or an optimist?"

"Neither," I quickly retorted, and just as I was about to tell him I was a realist, a new word came to me with the suddenness of certainty. "I'm a hopefulist."

Pessimism and optimism are both boxed-in ways of thinking. They form a finite continuum somewhere along which our general dispositions tend to hover. Most of us would claim neither end of the spectrum, preferring some version of realism. We like to call it a "third way." We frame it like a pragmatic compromise.

The psalmist shows us a different way. Rather than fretting endlessly in analysis over the pros and cons of this move or the other and the probable outcomes, the psalmist sings his way into the divine perspective. The psalmist refuses to ignore the reality that he is hiding in a cave. He will not put a nice face on a miserable circumstance and apparent defeat. He initially comes off as a pessimist. Neither does the singer succumb to the optimistic possibilities of conventional warfare. He refuses the overtures of positive thinking. He remembers God.

The Psalms simply do not exist on the two-dimensional human continuum of pessimism and optimism and realistic outcomes. These songs create another spectrum altogether. The tribe of the psalmist operates in the realm of memory and imagination. We remember what God has done. We imagine what he is capable of. We do not fret as to whether the odds are in our favor precisely because we are not betting on ourselves. The odds do not matter one whit to those who are already "all in." It is God with whom we deal, not our detractors or enemies.

Yes, I am a hopefulist.

"And He must win the battle."
—Martin Luther, "A Mighty Fortress Is Our God"

The psalmist teaches us the soundtrack of hope. Do we have the audacity to sing along?

Ask Yourself. Share with Another.

How about you? Are you a pessimist or an optimist? A realist? Do you grasp the distinction between these options and becoming a "hopefulist"? Do you grasp that "hopefulism" is not a fourth option or a middle way, but a complete paradigm shift? What would that look like for you?

Why Depression Is So Rampant

PSALM 10

MORNING SONG or KINGSFOLD   86.86 C.M.
Words by Timothy Tennent based on Psalm 10

1   Why, LORD, do You stand far away in times of trial
      and pain?
2   The wicked ones in arrogance afflict the weak
      for gain.

    The weak are caught in schemes they plan, the
      wicked boast indeed!
3   They're proud of cravings in their heart, they love the
      life of greed.

4   In his own pride he seeks Him not, the Lord's not in
      his mind,
5   He prospers in his haughtiness, Your laws he will
      not find.

6   The wicked sneers at all his foes, "Nothing will e'er
      shake me.
    I'll always know this happiness, and trouble I'll
      not see."

7   His mouth is full of lies and threats; evil is on
        his tongue.
8   He waits to ambush innocent, to murder old or young.

9   For victims he in secret waits, like lions wait for prey;
     They catch the helpless in their net, and drag them off
        to slay.

10   He crushes them and sees them fall, and does not
        hide in shame.
11   He says, "God has forgotten this, and on me there's
        no blame."

12   Arise, O LORD, lift up Your hand; forget not those
        in need!
13   Why, Lord, do they revile Your name, thinking You
        ne'er take heed?

14   But, You, O God, see all our grief; You take it all
        to mind;
     The victim knows You are his help, a father
        fath'rless find.

15   O, break the arm of evil men; call them before
        Your throne;
     May all their deeds come into light, in judgment they
        be known.

16   The LORD is King for evermore, the nations will
        not stand;
17   O LORD, You hear all of our cries, the needy in the land.

18   For You defend the fatherless; on sinners wrath
        You pour;
     So that the wicked of this earth may terrify no more.

Consider This . . .

He's at it again. Another bad day. Our singer finds himself back in the depths of despair . . . again. But again we must note his medication of choice: lament.[6]

In a world that values the pursuit of happiness above all else (and that misdefines happiness in every conceivable way), lament is a non-value. It is impossible to overestimate how much this pursuit of happiness shapes everything about us. The standard greeting of the day, "How are you doing?" is met with the standard answer, "Fine." (I once heard that response defined as an acronym for Frustrated, Insecure, Nervous, and Exhausted!)

I am becoming convinced that depression is so rampant precisely because lament is so repressed. Think about it. Years and years of life's ordinary disappointments, wounds, broken relationships, lost opportunities, sinful mistakes, grievous losses, deaths, and on we could go—unlamented, held inside, slowly repressed, and exiled to the Siberian wasteland of our souls. It's enough to permanently alter a person's internal brain chemistry. This is what causes so much depression.

Consider this: a full one-third of all of the Psalms (by my count fifty-eight) are songs of lament. It strikes me that we should assume that about one-third of our life is going to be a disappointing mess that many times cannot be resolved, only lamented. Might it be a revolutionary strategy to reset our expectations in light of this and to learn how to lament? Think about how this might impact the other two-thirds of our lives. It strikes me as another example of the counterintuitive logic of the cross. The way of death and resurrection . . . endings and beginnings.

This is the way song provides a subversive strategy in the face of sadness.

Ask Yourself. Share with Another.

What's the story of depression in your life? Ever experienced it? Do you still think it is an abnormal part of the human experience? Why or why not?

Sing it at soundtrack.seedbed.com

DAY 30

Why Queen's "We Are the Champions" Is Actually a Lament

PSALM 35

ST. MICHAEL, ST. THOMAS, TERRA BEATA, or SOUTHWELL   66.86 S.M.
Words by Julie Tennent based on Psalm 35

1   Contend, O Lord, with those who do contend with me;
    And fight against all those arrayed who battle
        against me.
2   Take up Your shield and sword; arise, come to my aid.
3   Oppose all those pursuing me; say to me, "You
        are saved."

4   May those who seek my life now be disgraced
        and shamed;
    May those who plot my ruin, Lord, be turned back
        and dismayed.
5   Like chaff before the wind, may angels drive
        them out.
6   May their path dark and slipp'ry be—pursued by
        angels' shout.

7   Because they hid their net, dug pits without a cause;

8   May nets they hid entangle them; in their pits let
        them fall.
9   Then my soul will rejoice in the LORD's salvation;
10   And I'll exclaim, "Who's like You, LORD? You save the
        poor from them."

11   The ruthless testify; pose questions filled with scorn;
12   They repay evil for my good and leave my
        soul forlorn.
13   And yet when they were ill, I fasted and I prayed;
14   I mourned as for my friend in grief, tears as for
        family made.

15   But when I fell, they came; attacked with
        sland'rous glee.
16   Like wicked, they with malice mocked, and gnashed
        their teeth at me.
17   How long will You look on? O Lord, come rescue me!
     And save my life from ravages of lions who stalk me.

18   Then I will give You thanks; Your praises I will sing;
     And in the congregation great, exalting praise
        I'll bring.
19   Don't let my foes rejoice, who hate me without cause.
     Don't let them gloat and wink their eye with malice,
        but no cause.

20   They do not speak in peace, but plan their wicked lies;
21   Against the peaceful, they say, "Ha! We've seen with
        our own eyes!"
22   But You, O LORD, have seen; don't be far off, O Lord.
23   Awake and rise to my defense; contend for me,
        my God.

24   LORD, in Your righteousness, don't let them gloat
        o'er me.

25 Don't let them think, "Aha, we won! We've conquered
      him wholly."
26 May those who gloat o'er me and the distress I face,
      Who lift themselves o'er me be clothed with shame
      and with disgrace.

27 May all who take delight that vindication's mine,
      May they with joy and gladness shout, and say, "The
      glory's Thine!"
      The LORD delights as those, His servants, are
      made strong;
28 My tongue will sing Your righteousness and praises all
      day long.

Consider This . . .

Freddy Mercury had it right. I am only now beginning
to understand that his song "We Are the Champions" is
actually a lament. He is claiming a victory that is already-
but-not-yet. The hope here is not so much in God, as it is
in the final score, but you get the point. As Peter Kuzmic,
a noted theologian from Croatia, is believed to have said,
"Hope is the ability to hear the music of the future. Faith
is having the courage to dance to it today." Look up the
lyrics to "We Are the Champions," and you'll see what
I mean.

Now, be honest. You couldn't resist singing along
as you read through it, could you? You could hear the
music, couldn't you? It would be an absurd exercise to
simply read the lyrics without music, wouldn't it?

The same is true of the Psalms—songs they are.

Ask Yourself. Share with Another.

Can you remember a time when you experienced some form of opposition? Our friends may provide helpful resistance to us, but an enemy outright opposes. The challenge is knowing the difference. Have you ever experienced having a friend who became an enemy?

You Will Never Know That God Is All You Need until You Know He's All You Have

. . . .

PSALM 41

ELLACOMBE, FOREST GREEN, or KINGSFOLD   86.86 C.M. D
Words by Timothy Tennent based on Psalm 41

1   How blessed is the one who loves the helpless and
        the weak;
     The LORD delivers and protects that one when
        troubles peak.
2   The LORD preserves and saves his life, and blesses in
        the land,
     He'll not surrender him to foes, but keep him in
        His hand.

3   The LORD sustains him when he's ill, and lifts him from
        his bed;
     The Lord his illness takes away by lifting up his head.
4   I said, "O LORD, have mercy on a sinner steeped
        in wrong;
     Heal me, O Lord, for I have sinned against You all
        day long."

5   My enemies about me say, with malice, ill intent,
     "When will he die? When will his name both perish
          and be spent?"
6   For everyone speaks ill of me and slanders in
          his heart;
     Then they go out and spread their lies; great evil
          they impart.

7   My enemies conspire and plot and set their traps
          for me;
     They whisper evil plans for me as if I cannot see.
8   They say, "A vile disease has come and struck him
          down to die;
     His bed will be his earthly end, right where he now
          does lie."

9   Even my friend who shared my bread, in whom I put
          my trust
     has lifted up his heel 'gainst me and scattered me
          with dust.
10   But You, O Lord, have mercy now and raise me up,
          I pray,
     That I may rise and turn on them and all their
          sins repay.

11   I know that You are pleased with me; my foes they will
          not stand;
12   In my integrity hold me, safe in Your righteous hand.
13   Praise be to God our cov'nant Lord, the God of Israel,
     Forever and forevermore. Amen, Amen we'll tell!

Consider This . . .

There's an old saying that comes to mind in light of today's song: "You will never know that God is all you need until you know he's all you have."

We might classify today's song as a lament for the sick. The singer has come down with something pretty bad, but it's actually worse than that. His enemies are gloating over his condition and seem to be circling above his hospital bed like vultures. Others of his detractors whisper slander, stoking the fires of the rumor mill. Even worse than that, one of the singer's friends turns on him. And we are given the impression it isn't one of his so-called "friends." This is a close, personal friend, a trusted confidant who has defected and gone to the dark side. Note how the song phrases it:

> Even my friend who shared my bread, in whom I put my trust,
> has lifted up his heel 'gainst me, and scattered me with dust.

The image to hold in mind here is that of a rider being thrown from his most cherished horse, only to then be kicked in the face by the horse when he's down.

There's another image that comes to mind here:

"Jesus answered, 'It is the one to whom I will give this piece of bread when I have dipped it in the dish.' Then, dipping the piece of bread, he gave it to Judas, the son of Simon Iscariot" (John 13:26).

And yes, it gets worse still. This trusted friend had effectively turned Jesus over to the police. And just when you thought it couldn't get any worse, this bread-sharing buddy betrayed him with a kiss. And that's probably about the worst of it. Truth be told, this single act of treachery probably hurt him more than all the torture of Friday ever did.

As these days of Lent process us to Jerusalem, the way of lament keeps taking us further and further into descent. And yes, bad as this present situation is, it will get worse before it gets better. But our great worship leader, Jesus, shows us what it looks like to sing our way through.

He is going to take us to the place where it might be said, "You will never know that God is all you need until you know he's all you have."

That's when we will know what it really means to sing. Practice now.

Ask Yourself. Share with Another.

Do you have a story of betrayal? Did it come at the hands of a friend? Have you forgiven them? Maybe it's because you haven't lamented the situation before God? This kind of thing can really handicap the soul. Is it time to break free?

Sing it at soundtrack.seedbed.com

On War and Peace

. . . .

PSALM 120

MORNING SONG   86.86 C.M.
Words by Julie Tennent based on Psalm 120

1   I call the LORD in my distress
    and He does answer me.
2   O save me, LORD, from lying lips
    and tongues that speak deceit.

3   What will He do to you, O tongue,
    Deceitful as you be?
4   He'll punish you with arrows sharp
    and coals of the broom tree.

5   O, woe to me, that I must dwell
    in Meshech, Keder's land!
6   Too long I've lived among the ones
    who peace don't understand.

7   For I am one who longs for peace,
    But they do peace abhor.
    When I speak of my heart for peace,
    They only are for war.

Consider This . . .

It's no coincidence that right after Jesus said, "Blessed are the peacemakers," he said, "Blessed are those who are persecuted because of righteousness" (Matt. 5:9–10). Why do people dislike peacemakers? Perhaps the better question might be: Why do they love war? Be it current events, politics, or church splits, people seem to thrive on conflict.

Think of it this way. In life we see two primary centers of gravity: war and peace. People tend to be caught in one or another of those gravitational pulls. The unfortunate default state of the human race is the state of war. In the beginning, when God created the heavens and the earth, all of creation enjoyed the peace of God. The fundamental character of peace is that of deep contentment. The fundamental character of war is discontentedness. Adam and Eve demonstrated a discontentment with the state of perfect peace when they chose to disobey God. The result was war. At the core of the ensuing curse came conflict—between men and women, between people and creation, and between creation and God. War, in its essence, is the concentrated, accumulated impact of sin. War uncreates creation. Peace makes creation new again. War can be declared in an instant through the breaking of a relationship. Peace must be worked out through the mending of relationship (and it often takes time). War is the absence of peace. However, peace is not the absence of war. Peace is the presence of God, which is why peace is able to thrive in the midst of the worst angst and anxiety imaginable. It's why they call it the peace that passes all understanding.

God sent his Son, the Prince of Peace, into the warring factions of his creation and the result was the persecution of crucifixion. Peace won out though. On the third day he was raised from the dead. After his resurrection he gathered with his followers and said to them, "'Peace be with you! As the Father has sent me, I am sending you.' And with that he breathed on them and said, 'Receive the Holy Spirit'" (John 20.21–22).

So there's the story of war and peace. Peacemakers need a song. We get that today in Song 120.

Ask Yourself. Share with Another.

War is the absence of peace, but peace is not the absence of war. Do you grasp the truth in this statement? Identify situations in your life where the conflict may be passed but peace still eludes you. Do you want peace or are you satisfied with an uneasy truce?

Sing it at soundtrack.seedbed.com

DAY 33

This Is a Psalm
for Every Day

· ·

PSALM 121

DUNDEE, NEW BRITAIN, or AZMON   86.86 C.M.
Words by Julie Tennent based on Psalm 121

1   I lift my eyes up to the hills—
    Where does my help find birth?
2   My help comes from the LORD who made
    the heavens and the earth.

3   He will not let your foot to slip;
    His watch o'er you He keeps;
4   The Lord who watches Israel,
    He slumbers not nor sleeps.

5   The LORD keeps vigil over you,
    He's shade at your right hand.
6   Not sun nor moon will harm you, but
    by day and night you'll stand.

7   The LORD will keep you from all harm;
    Your life He does restore.
8   The LORD will watch you come and go
    both now and evermore.

Consider This . . .

I've written about Song 121 before. It's one of my favorites.

While many of the Psalms deal with particular kinds of circumstances, I think of Song 121 as an everyday psalm. Every single day, at the forefront of my mind, I want the following to be real in my everyday experience:

> My help comes from the Lord, the maker of heaven and earth.
> He will not let me lose my footing.
> He will not go to sleep at the wheel.
> He will keep me.
> He is my shade.
> He is my protection.
> He will deliver me from evil.
> He will hold my life together.
> He will watch over me with all my comings and my goings.

This gives me confidence. I need not worry. He has me. That's enough.

And can I recommend you sing this one song to the tune "New Britain"? You will find you already know it by heart. (It's the tune to "Amazing Grace.")

Ask Yourself. Share with Another.

So do you have an everyday psalm? If not, it's time to get one. What would it be? And what will be your cue or trigger to sing it? For me, I sing this one when I tie my shoes.

The Tragic Irony of Those Gates of Jerusalem

· ·

PSALM 122

PENITENTIA or MORECAMBE   10.10.10.10
Words by Julie Tennent based on Psalm 122

1   I was so glad when they said unto me,
    "Come, let's go to the house of God the Lord."
2   Our feet are standing here within your gates,
    O bless'd Jerusalem, of all adored.

3   See now Jerusalem, the city great,
    Built as a city close—compacted well;
4   To which the tribes go up—tribes of the Lord,
    To praise His name, as He told Israel.

5   There were the thrones for judgment set by God;
    The thrones of David who ruled all the land;
6   Pray for the peace now of Jerusalem,
    "May all who love you prosper well, and stand."

7   "May there be peace within your walls always;
    Prosperity within your citadels."
8   So for the sake of brothers and of friends,
    And for the sake of all of Israel;

Thus, I will say, "May peace within you reign."
9   And for the sake of the house of the Lord,
     I will seek your prosperity and good,
     O bless'd Jerusalem, of all adored.

Consider This . . .

We find ourselves now walking through the final weeks with Jesus on this desert journey to Jerusalem. Lazarus's resurrection party is now in the rearview mirror. The time for pilgrimage has come again. We march to Zion—beautiful, beautiful Zion. We hear the litany spoken across the throngs of pilgrims.

The great call, "I was glad when they said unto me," met with the resounding response, "Let us go into the house of the Lord" (see Psalm 122:1 KJV).

We are here, Jerusalem! Standing within your gates! And all we have heard of this marvelous place is true. You, Jerusalem, our citadel. We pray for your peace. In your peace we find our own.

The stage is set for the final weeks. Come Sunday, the throngs will wave their palm branches as the Nazarene enters the city on the back of a donkey. The King of kings comes into the great city of kings. Yes! We will agree, "Blessed is he who comes in the name of the Lord" (Matt. 21:9). Soon we will find ourselves in a second-floor room of an obscure house in the middle of the city, sharing a meal that will be known to all of history as the Last Supper. Who could know that the cosmic drama of redemption would play out in such a way? Behind it all we hear the echo of the Baptist's voice, "Behold, the Lamb of God, who takes away the sin of the world!" (John 1:29 ESV).

"Jerusalem, Jerusalem," [the Lamb will cry out,] "you who kill the prophets and stone those sent to you, how often I have longed to gather your children together, as a hen gathers her chicks under her wings, and you were not willing" (Luke 13:34).

Irony of ironies: the Peace of Jerusalem, himself, comes into Jerusalem. He will pass through her gates lifted on the accolades of great acclaim; only to be led back through them slammed under the shame of withering scorn.

We are here! Jerusalem! Standing within your very gates!

Maranatha! (It means "Come, O Lord!")

Sing now.

Ask Yourself. Share with Another.

Can you allow this psalm to lead you into the drama of our great history; the story of this tortured city, Jerusalem? Will you stand within the gates of this ancient, cosmic place of God's mysterious working?

Sing it at soundtrack.seedbed.com

DAY 35

The Song of the Betrayed, or, What to Sing in the Face of Betrayal

PSALM 55

ABERYSTWYTH   77.77 D
Words by Julie Tennent based on Psalm 55

1   Listen to my prayer, O God,
    And do not ignore my plea;
2   Hear and answer, for my thoughts
    do dismay and trouble me,
3   At the voice of enemies,
    At the stares of wicked ones;
    They bring suff'ring down on me,
    Their sharp taunt is never done.

4   My heart is in anguish sore,
    Death's great terror assails me;
5   Fear and trembling plague me more,
    Horror has o'ertaken me.
6   I said, "Oh, that I could fly
    far away and be at rest!

7   I would flee far as the sky,
8   Shelter far from storm's tempest."

9   Lord, confuse them and confound
    words they speak and deeds they do;
    Violent strife is all around
    in the city through and through.
10 Day and night they prowl about
    on its walls and all within;
11 They destroy and loot and rout,
    Streets are filled with lies and sin.

12 If a foe or enemy
    insults me, I'll take from him
    anything he says 'gainst me;
    I could hide myself from him.
13 But it's you, my closest friend;
14 You with whom I walked abroad,
    Had sweet friendship without end,
    Even in the house of God.

15 Let death take my enemies
    by surprise, their life grow dim;
    Let the grave their life now seize—
    Evil finds its home with them.
16 But I call to God alone,
    The LORD saves me in distress;
17 Evening, morning, and at noon,
    I cry out—He hears, gives rest.

18 He will ransom me unharmed
    from the battle waged 'gainst me;
    Though I was opposed, alarmed,
    Though my foes were vast, many.
19 God, who is enthroned always
    will afflict them with His rod;

For they never change their ways
and they have no fear of God.

20 My companion sacks his friends,
     Violates his covenant;
     His attacking never ends,
     Evil from his heart is sent.
21 Speech is smooth as butter sweet,
     But his heart is only war;
     Words are soothing he repeats,
     But they carry a drawn sword.

22 Cast your cares upon the LORD;
     He'll sustain you when you call.
     He will ever keep His word,
     Never let the righteous fall.
23 But God, You will act always
     to bring wicked ones their due;
     They won't live out half their days,
     As for me, I trust in You.

Consider This . . .

Song 55 offers us the sad rehearsal for the garden of
Gethsemane, the fated garden of betrayal.

Anyone who has experienced betrayal knows the pain
of this song. It brings pure anguish, dread, overwhelming
sadness, and yes, anger. Song 55 is bitter medicine for the
betrayed; yet it is pure gall for the traitor. The sentence
for betraying one's country is death, but the punishment
for one who betrays a friend is far worse. It is suicide.
Betrayal is an irreversible wound both because of the way
it injures the one betrayed and for the sad way it destroys

the betrayer. Adultery is a form of betrayal. While devastating for the one betrayed, it inflicts intractable pain on the adulterer. Betrayal is a form of adultery without the solace of another lover.

Get a picture in your mind of Judas Iscariot hanging from the tree, swinging back and forth like the pendulum of a clock that will never stop ticking. We hear it to the present day. The problem with Judas is not that he could not be forgiven and even reconciled. It is that he could not forgive himself.

I think this is the compassionate source of Jesus' words to Judas, "Do what you have to do" (see John 13:27), and of his prayer, "Father, forgive them, for they know not what they do" (Luke 23:34 ESV). The betrayer willfully wraps herself in the warrant of her difficult act. At the same time she unwittingly wraps herself in an inescapable straitjacket of self-justification such that it ultimately destroys her.

The problem with Judas is he never got to see the tragic mercy of the cross. For at the same time the Betrayed One bore the wounds of betrayal, he also took on himself the wounds of the betrayer. The mystery of redemption is how the Betrayed One will offer up his own life for the sake of the betrayer, who took his own life.

This is perhaps the most difficult place of the cross. It is too deep to fathom. We can only behold.

It is time to practice the song now. Gethsemane is just around the corner.

Ask Yourself. Share with Another.

Are you ready to let go of your betrayers; to release them? Are you ready to forgive the debt they owe you, even if they never own up to it? Watch how Jesus does it. Follow him.

The Secret of the Penitential Psalms: There Are Only Two Laws

. . . .

PSALM 130

MORNING SONG   86.86 C.M.
Words by Julie Tennent based on Psalm 130

1 Out of the depths I cry to You,
2 O Lord, now hear my voice!
   Let Your ears be attentive to
   my cry for mercy voiced.

3 If You, O Lord, recorded sins,
   Then who, O Lord, could stand?
4 But with You there forgiveness is—
   Therefore, we fear Your hand.

5 I wait for God, my soul does wait;
   His word's my hope and stay;
6 My soul waits for the Lord more than
   the watchmen wait for day.

   Yes, more than watchmen wait for morn,
   I wait for God above.

7   O Israel, put hope in this:
    The LORD's unfailing love.

    For with the LORD is steadfast love,
    Redemption full and free;
8   For He will redeem Israel,
    From all iniquity.

Consider This . . .

This morning, before school, I managed to find a few
minutes to spend talking about the goodness of God
with at least two of my four children: 2 out of 4 before
7:00 a.m. = a good day. I shared with my two girls a bold
assertion. Namely, there are only two basic rules or laws
in the universe: 1) the law of sin and death; and 2) the law
of the Spirit of life. How did I decide on this, you ask? I
typically open up the Bible app on my iPhone, and under
the "Today" tab it will always offer one Bible scripture of
the day. Today's scripture was Romans 8:1–2, which says,
"Therefore, there is now no condemnation for those who
are in Christ Jesus, because through Christ Jesus the law
of the Spirit who gives life has set you free from the law
of sin and death."

I love the binary nature of texts like these. I shared
with my daughters the unfortunate news that because of
Adam and Eve's failure to "make better choices" (tech-
nical term used on behavior clip charts at school), we
were all born into and under the law of sin and death.
But, because of Jesus, who was a "Super Student" (tech-
nical term for the very top of the behavior clip charts at

school), we were set free from the law of sin and death by the law of the Spirit. In other words, just as we were born into the law of sin and death, we can be born a second time by the law of the Spirit into life, which is freedom from the law of sin and death. Just as it was that by no fault of our own we were born into the law of sin and death, so it was that by no act of our own we could be born into the life-giving law of the Spirit.

Don't hear me wrong here. Just because we did nothing in and of ourselves to be born into the law of sin and death doesn't mean that we haven't earned the right to live there. Because we are subject to that law, we cannot help but live according to it. As I've said before, we are not sinners because we sin. We sin because we are sinners. Confession is simply the act of coming to terms with the law of sin and death and becoming honest about all the bad outcomes it has led to in our life. That's what the seven confession songs (a.k.a. penitential psalms) do—they bring it all down to the only two laws.

Here's the gospel. The corollary of the law of sin and death is even more true. As we are subject to the life-giving law of the Spirit, we cannot help but live according to it. In other words, sin has lost its power. These confession songs, engaged over time, process us out of the law of sin and death and into the law of the Spirit of life.

Go back and sing through Song 130 again, noting these realities. It's a game changer. We are no longer looking at our clip chart on the chalkboard of life. We get to look at Jesus' clip chart. His chart says, "No condemnation!"

So if you are having trouble singing, how about turning on the music and just reading the words aloud in time with the song. It will make a difference.

Ask Yourself. Share with Another.

I know you have discovered the law of sin and death. Have you also discovered the law of the Spirit of life or, said differently, the life-giving law of the Spirit? Are you ready? Ask Jesus now to lead you into this reality as the new law of your life. He will do it.

Sing it at soundtrack.seedbed.com

DAY 37

Here's a Great Idea for the Chorus to the Song Your Life Is Writing

. . . .

PSALM 124

BEECHER, ODE TO JOY, or NETTLETON   87.87
Words by Julie Tennent based on Psalm 124

1 If the LORD had not been with us—O, let Israel now say;
2 If the LORD had not been with us, when we were
       amidst the fray.
3 When attackers in their anger would have put us in
       the grave;
4 Torrents would have there engulfed us;
5 raging floods swept us away.

6 Blessed be the LORD who has not let us be torn from
       His care;
7 Like a bird, we have escaped from out the angry
       fowler's snare.
   For the snare has now been broken; we've escaped as
       like new birth;
8 Our help's in the name of Yahweh, Maker of the heav'n
       and earth.

Consider This . . .

"If the LORD had not been with us . . ."

Do you remember Abraham? Or Moses? Or the Red Sea? Do you remember Miriam? Or Jericho? How about Gideon? Or Ruth? Or Goliath? Do you remember Rahab? Do you remember Hezekiah? How about Josiah? Do you remember Nehemiah? Or Jeremiah? What about Isaiah? Jonah? Daniel? Do you remember Elijah? How about Mary? Do you remember Peter? Do you remember Paul?

These men and women, these stories, all have one thing in common. To a person, Song 124 sits near the top of their most frequent playlist.

The following words could well preface just about anything they would be apt to talk about: "If the LORD had not been with us . . ."

So do you remember these stories? These are just a few of the stories that matter. They are the stories that are the substance of the Psalms, the stories behind the soundtrack. These are the stories to impress on our hearts and to teach to our children and to talk about when we get up and when we lie down and when we walk along the road (see Deuteronomy 6:7; 11:19). It is not enough to know these stories. We must remember them, actively, all the time. These are our stories. They keep our faith centered in God rather than in our own determination and drive.

As we remember these "If the LORD had not been with us . . ." stories, we will begin to add to them our own.

So how about you? What are your "If the LORD had not been with us . . ." songs? Your life is writing a song, you know. This makes for a great chorus to your verses.

We have a great melody for this one ready for you. Does Beethoven's "Ode to Joy" ring a bell?

Ask Yourself. Share with Another.

Have you begun to collect your own album of "If the LORD had not been with us . . ." stories? Think of one now. Now do an Internet search for "Here I raise my Ebenezer" to learn more.

DAY 38

The Three Most-Prayed Words in the World— and a Better Idea

. . . .

PSALM 125

SOUTHWELL or ST. THOMAS   66.86 S.M.
Words by Julie Tennent based on Psalm 125

1   Those who trust in the LORD
     are like Mount Zion's hill
     which can't be shaken, but endures
     forever firmly still.

2   As mountains do surround
     your walls, Jerusalem;
     The LORD surrounds His people now,
     And evermore keeps them.

3   The reign of wicked ones
     will not remain or stand,
     Over the place allotted to
     the righteous and their land.

     For then the righteous might
     do evil with their hand;

4   Do good, O Lᴏʀᴅ, to those good ones
     who for the upright stand.

5   But those who turn aside
     to crooked, evil ways;
     The Lᴏʀᴅ will banish with all wrong—
     Peace for all Isr'el's days.

Consider This . . .

Of all the prayers God hears every day, what kind of prayers do you think he hears the most? My hunch is he mostly hears a prayer that comes down to about three words, "Keep us safe." Next to food, water, and shelter, human beings crave safety and security. Yes, I'd say people pray for safety more than just about anything else. Am I right?

Like a number of others, Song 125 offers a different strategy from anxious prayers for safety. Instead of praying for safety, this song declares protection. It states security. "As the mountains surround Jerusalem, so the Lᴏʀᴅ surrounds his people" (v. 2). Not only that, it projects images of protection and security. Note, the song doesn't say, "God keeps us safe." The song reaches for an image of protection and leads us to sing into that picture. That's what metaphors are for. They cause the soul to think. To declare that God keeps us safe is a truth, but it keeps things at the level of knowledge. To declare, "As the mountains surround Jerusalem, so the Lᴏʀᴅ surrounds his people"—now, that's a vision!

Faith requires a comprehension beyond mere knowledge of truth. Faith is far more about seeing a vision than possessing knowledge.

The more our songs declare protection, the less we will find ourselves praying for safety. There's just a lot more pressing agendas that need our prayers—like praying for a great awakening to the gospel in this land and beyond, or praying for the persecuted or the poor, and on we could go.

Sure, praying for safety is fine. But might declaring God's protection be a bolder strategy? I say go for it!

And instead of telling one another to be safe, how about we start encouraging one another to be bold!

And don't just say it—sing it.

Ask Yourself. Share with Another.

Are you ready to get beyond the "safe" confines of prayers for safety? How about the approach of the psalmist to declare protection around yourself and those you love? Will you try that? As the mountains surround Jerusalem, so does the Lord surround [insert your people here].

Sing it at soundtrack.seedbed.com

The Promise of Joy in the Desert

. . . .

PSALM 110

FOUNDATION or ST. DENIO   11.11.11.11
Words by Julie Tennent based on Psalm 110

1   The Lord said to my Lord, "Sit at My right hand;
     Until all your enemies no more can stand.
     I'll make them a footstool for under your feet."
2   And you'll rule from Zion—your vict'ry complete.

3   Your troops will be willing on your battle day;
     They will be majestic in holy array.
     From dawn's early womb, they will serve you in truth,
     They'll be like the dew in the prime of their youth.

4   The Lord God has sworn and will not change His mind:
     You're a priest forever of a unique kind.
     Your priesthood is not like the one you have known;
     Melchizedek's order is both priest and throne.

5   The Lord's at your right hand—He'll crush kings in wrath.
6   He'll judge all the nations—the dead fill His path.
     He'll crush all earth's kings. When to brooks He is led,
7   He'll drink peacefully and will lift up His head.

142

Consider This . . .

Down through the ages of the church, Song 110 has often been considered the crown jewel of the whole songbook. From the ancient Trinitarian allusions to the order of Melchizedek, to the final judgment, Song 110 is layered with messianic prophecies, now fulfilled by Jesus.

Charles H. Spurgeon, in *The Treasury of David: Classic Reflections on the Wisdom of the Psalms,* quotes the great reformer Martin Luther, who called Psalm 110 "a well-spring—nay, a treasury of all Christian doctrines, understanding, wisdom, and comfort, richer and fuller than any other passage of Holy Writ."[7]

Continuing on Song 110, Spurgeon goes on to quote Augustine's description, "'*verbis brevis, sensu infinitus,*' short in words, but in sense infinite."[8]

The psalm puts us in touch with "the joy set before us," as we travel the desert path home (see Hebrews 12:2).

When you sing this one, remember: you are singing with Luther and Augustine and, yes, Jesus.

Ask Yourself. Share with Another.

Is the season in which you are living coinciding with the season of Lent? If so, then you are riding this train all the way to Jerusalem. If not, you can get off at this station. But the station of the cross is good for any season. You've come this far. It would be good for your soul to ride it out.

SUNDAY: PASSION WEEK

Is Your Understanding of the Passion of Jesus Arrested in Development?

. . . .

PSALM 118

KINGSFOLD or FOREST GREEN   86.86 C.M. D
Words by Julie Tennent based on Psalm 118

1   O praise the LORD, for He is good; His love
    endures always;
2   Let those of Israel now say, "His love endures always."
3   And let the house of Aaron say, "His love
    endures always."
4   Let those who fear the LORD now say, "His love
    endures always."

5   In my distress, I called the LORD, and He did
    answer me;
    I cried in anguish, and He heard—from trouble set
    me free.
6   The LORD is with me, ever sure; I will not be afraid;
    For what is there that man can do, when I am on
    Him stayed?

7   The Lord's with me; He is my help against
        the enemy;
    Therefore, upon all of my foes I'll look triumphantly.
8   It's better far to trust the Lord than trust in
        man's defense;
9   To find your refuge in the Lord than trust in king
        or prince.

10 The nations have surrounded me; they compass
        me about;
    But in the Lord's most holy name, I shall them all
        root out.
11 They came around on every side; they compassed
        me about;
    But in the Lord's most holy name, I shall them all
        root out.

12 They swarmed around me like fierce bees, like dry
        thorns set aflame;
    They quickly died out, for I cut them off in the
        Lord's name.
13 They pushed me back so that I fell, but then the Lord
        helped me;
14 The Lord is both my strength and song; and my
        salvation He.

15 In dwellings of the righteous ones is heard the
        joyous shout;
    The Lord's right hand does mighty things, salvation
        brings about.
16 The right hand of the mighty Lord is lifted up
        on high;
    The Lord's right hand does mighty things, and so I
        shall not die.

17 I shall not die, but live and tell His works with
    every breath;
18 The LORD has chastened me, but has not giv'n me o'er
    to death.
19 Now open unto me the gates, the gates
    of righteousness;
    Then I will enter into them, and ever the LORD bless.

20 This is the gate of the LORD God; the just shall
    enter there;
21 I will give thanks—You answered me and my
    salvation prayer.
22 That stone is made head cornerstone which builders
    did despise;
23 This is the doing of the LORD, and wondrous in
    our eyes.

24 This is the day the LORD has made; rejoice exceedingly;
25 O save us, LORD; grant us success, and send prosperity.
26 For blessed is the one who comes in the name of
    the LORD;
    From the LORD's house, we bless you now—where
    blessing is outpoured.

27 The LORD is God, and He has made His light on us
    to rise;
    Bind to the altar's horns with cords the festal sacrifice.
28 You are my God; I'll give You thanks, exalt You all
    my days;
29 O praise the LORD, for He is good; His love
    endures always.

Consider This . . .

> Jesus took the Twelve aside and told them, "We are going up to Jerusalem, and everything that is written by the prophets about the Son of Man will be fulfilled. He will be delivered over to the Gentiles. They will mock him, insult him and spit on him; they will flog him and kill him. On the third day he will rise again."
>
> The disciples did not understand any of this. Its meaning was hidden from them, and they did not know what he was talking about. (Luke 18:31–34)

We must remember always: you and I are, at best, those disciples who "did not understand any of this." We cannot allow ourselves to be lulled into the so-called benefit of hindsight. Holy Week is ever before us. Sure, we may understand all of this at a historical level, and we may even grasp the doctrinal implications of his Passion, but here's the question I am asking myself: Is my understanding of the meaning of his Passion growing, or has it become arrested in development somewhere along the way?

What I'm saying may seem somewhat abstract to you, but we will be well served to remember that at the heart of it all is pure mystery. As we enter into the Passion of Jesus, let us join together and affirm with the church at all times and in all places the Great Mystery of our faith: Christ has died! Christ is risen! Christ *will come again*!

Ask Yourself. Share with Another.

Is my understanding of the meaning of his Passion growing, or has it become arrested in development somewhere along the way? No matter how many times you may have walked this journey to Jerusalem before, every time it's different. Open yourself up for new revelations. Humble yourself in the sight of the Lord.

MONDAY OF PASSION WEEK

BOOM! Goes the Dynamite

. . . .

PSALM 31

SWEET HOUR or GUIDANCE   88.88 L.M. D
Words by Julie Tennent based on Psalm 31

1   In You, O Lord, I refuge take, let me be never put
        to shame;
      And in Your righteousness, O Lord, deliver me—I trust
        Your name.
2   O Lord, turn now Your ear to me; come quickly and
        my rescue be;
      And be my rock of refuge sure, a fortress strong to
        rescue me.

3   Since You're my fortress and my rock, for Your name's
        sake, lead me and guide,
4   Free me from traps they set for me, for You're the
        Rock where I abide.
5   For I commit my spirit, Lord, into Your sovereign,
        loving hands;
      Redeem me, Lord, O God of truth; my life before You
        ever stands.

6   I hate those who to idols cling; I trust in God
        the Lord alone;

7   I will be glad and will rejoice in Your love, for I am
          Your own.
      For You saw my affliction and You knew the anguish
          of my soul;

8   Gave me not to my enemies, but set my feet in
          places full.

9   Be merciful to me, O Lord, for I am in distress
          and grief;
      My soul and body filled with grief; my eyes with
          sorrow do grow weak.

10   My life's consumed by anguish, Lord; my years by
          groans as You I seek;
      My strength fails from affliction, Lord; my very bones
          grow sick and weak.

11   Because of all my enemies, my neighbors pour
          contempt on me;
      I am a dread e'en to my friends—when they see me,
          they turn and flee.

12   I am forgotten as though dead; I'm like old
          broken pottery;

13   I hear their slander; fear fills me, for they conspire and
          plot 'gainst me.

14   But I do trust in You, O Lord; I say, "You are my
          God indeed."

15   My times are in Your hands for sure; deliver me
          from enemies.

16   Let Your face shine upon Your child; in Your unfailing
          love save me;

17   And let me not be put to shame, for I have cried
          out, Lord, to Thee.

17b Let shame upon the wicked come; let them lie silent
          in the grave;

18   Let lying lips be silenced, LORD; with pride and
        arrogance they rave.
19   How great Your goodness which You store for those
        who fear and reverence You;
     Which You bestow in sight of all on those who refuge
        take in You.

20   For in the shelter of Your wings, You hide them from
        intrigues of men;
     You keep them in Your dwelling place; safe from
        accusing tongues of men
21   Praise to the LORD, for He has shown His love when I
        was under siege;
22   In my alarm, I said, "O LORD, I'm cut off and You don't
        see me!"

22b Yet, LORD, You heard my cry for help; my cry for mercy
        You did hear;
23   O love the LORD, all you His saints! The LORD saves
        faithful who draw near.
     But all the proud He pays in full; He pays them back
        their due reward;
24   Be strong, O faithful, and take heart; all you who put
        hope in the LORD.

Consider This . . .

We know Jesus knew Song 31 by heart. He sang its core
affirmation from the cross, "Father, into your hands I
commit my spirit" (Luke 23:46).

     He had practiced this song from his youth. These
words grooved his deepest inner life. The singing of this
song (and the other 149) over and over again throughout

his life trained him in the unconventional warfare of the Spirit.

I can't overemphasize how essential it is for us who follow him to develop a fluency in this most holy language of prayer. At times it will seem routine, uninteresting, unspiritual, disconnected, and even meaningless . . . do it anyway! (This is how it is learning a new language. We never see those defining moments coming, yet on them so much rests.) The Psalms ready us for a response we never imagined was in us. It is a beautiful, powerful thing.

Take a look at Song 31 again. At perhaps the most pressing and dire moment in the war that was his life, he expressed the essence of 31 (indeed, that of the whole Psalter) in these words: "*Abba*, Father, . . . everything is possible for you. Take this cup from me. Yet not what I will, but what you will" (Mark 14:36).

Think about it—all 150 Psalms—right there.

BOOM! goes the dynamite. That's a game winner, every time.

Your turn to sing. And sing it as if your life depends on it. It well may.

Ask Yourself. Share with Another.

Can you press past the need to *feel* spiritual in working through these psalms? Remember, this is preparing your soul for the way ahead. Sometimes we must give up the need for warm fuzzies if we are to press on to deeper depths of faith.

TUESDAY OF PASSION WEEK

Holy Misnomer, Batman!

. . . .

ZECHARIAH 9:9

Rejoice greatly, O daughter of Zion!
Shout *in triumph*, O daughter of Jerusalem!
Behold, your king is coming to you;
He is just and endowed with salvation,
Humble, and mounted on a donkey,
Even on a colt, the foal of a donkey. (NASB)

Consider This . . .

Before we get too much further into Passion Week, I
want to revisit what I consider to be a major misnomer
we often find in our Bibles. *Misnomer*—it comes from a
French word that means "to wrongly name." Remember
back a few days ago with me to Palm Sunday, and the day
Jesus rode into Jerusalem "humble, and mounted on a
donkey," as the prophecy read.

Anyone remember the two words that appear in most
of our (English) Bibles as the heading over this passage
of Scripture? (See Matthew 21:1–17; Mark 11:1–11;

Luke 19:28–40; John 12:12–19.) Here is the misnomer: "Triumphal Entry."

These subheads, mind you, are not the Word of God. They are, rather, the work of translators. Likely, the translators were themselves playing with the irony. I will leave that to those smarter than I. Suffice it to say, though, this word "triumphal" is precisely the wrong word. Yes, it's the word we want and like, but it's wrong. Why not the "Humble Entry" or at least the "Prophetic Entry"?

Entries matter a lot. Just in case we entered this week with any notion of triumphal, as in "We Will Rock You" in our spirits, there's still time to run back outside the gates and come in again. Crawl this time.

Passion Week is not our annual opportunity to put yet another exclamation point on our theological dogmas and doctrinal foundations. Passion Week is the annual invitation to become disoriented by the holy love of God, shaken to the core of our comfortable being, and dispossessed of our sentimental illusions about grace.

For all practical purposes, the best two-word caption I can think of for all that is about to unfold? "Hell Week." The only one making a triumphal entry into Jerusalem was Satan himself. This is the week that the very gates of hell were opened, unleashing all hell on the Son of God. Remember that time in the desert when we were told that after unsuccessfully unseating Jesus with his tawdry temptations, "he left him until an opportune time" (Luke 4:13)?

This is that time.

Were you there when they crucified my Lord?
Were you there when they crucified my Lord?

O! Sometimes it causes me to tremble! tremble!
  tremble!
Were you there when they crucified my Lord?

Were you there when they nailed him to the cross?
Were you there when they nailed him to the cross?
O! Sometimes it causes me to tremble! tremble!
  tremble!
Were you there when they nailed him to the cross?

("Were You There?" American Spiritual, first printed in 1899)

Ask Yourself. Share with Another.

Am I growing? How?

Sing it at soundtrack.seedbed.com

WEDNESDAY OF PASSION WEEK

Undercover Boss Visits Headquarters

. . . .

LUKE 2:21-35; 19:45-48

On the eighth day, when it was time to circumcise the child, he was named Jesus, the name the angel had given him before he was conceived.

When the time came for the purification rites required by the Law of Moses, Joseph and Mary took him to Jerusalem to present him to the Lord (as it is written in the Law of the Lord, "Every firstborn male is to be consecrated to the Lord"), and to offer a sacrifice in keeping with what is said in the Law of the Lord: "a pair of doves or two young pigeons."

Now there was a man in Jerusalem called Simeon, who was righteous and devout. He was waiting for the consolation of Israel, and the Holy Spirit was on him. It had been revealed to him by the Holy Spirit that he would not die before he had seen the Lord's Messiah. Moved by the Spirit, he went into the temple courts. When the parents brought in the child Jesus to do for him what the custom of the Law required, Simeon took him in his arms and praised God, saying:

"Sovereign Lord, as you have promised,
    you may now dismiss your servant in peace.
For my eyes have seen your salvation,
    which you have prepared in the sight of all nations:
a light for revelation to the Gentiles,
    and the glory of your people Israel."

The child's father and mother marveled at what was said about him. Then Simeon blessed them and said to Mary, his mother: "This child is destined to cause the falling and rising of many in Israel, and to be a sign that will be spoken against, so that the thoughts of many hearts will be revealed. And a sword will pierce your own soul too." (Luke 2:21–35)

When Jesus entered the temple courts, he began to drive out those who were selling. "It is written," he said to them, "'My house will be a house of prayer'; but you have made it 'a den of robbers.'"

Every day he was teaching at the temple. But the chief priests, the teachers of the law and the leaders among the people were trying to kill him. Yet they could not find any way to do it, because all the people hung on his words. (Luke 19:45–48)

Consider This . . .

I wonder if his mom and dad told him. Did they share with Jesus at some right moment the words spoken over him on his eighth day by Simeon at the temple? Somehow, I think he remembered what he was too young to recall.

I bet he also remembered that "third day" in his twelfth year as his parents finally found him sitting in the temple courts, conversing with the rabbis. His response to his mom and dad was unforgettable: "'Why were you searching for me?' he asked. 'Didn't you know I had to be in my Father's house?'" (Luke 2:49).

He lived in Nazareth, but the temple was home for him. He came with the real blueprints for this majestic edifice because, in fact, he was himself the blueprint for the temple. The building plan himself had finally entered the building. As the Son of David, he, along with his disciples, ate the consecrated bread from the altar. As Jehovah Rapha, the Lord our Healer, he valiantly healed the sick in the temple, and as Lord of the Sabbath, he did it on the Sabbath.

On that day in the last week, the holy week that was hell week, the day he went first-century postal on the money changers in the temple—he was just putting the final touches on his renovation project.

Here is the One greater than the temple, the very Holy of Holies himself, who said, "Destroy this temple, and I will raise it again in three days" (John 2:19).

The perfection of his comprehensive revelation is breathtaking. The Lord of the Passover is about to become the Passover Lamb. Everything in heaven and on earth comes together in this week of all weeks. The very Word of God, sharper than a double-edged sword, will become the Pierced One.

The Passion of Jesus is the collision of cosmic chaos with creative love. It will unfold in a garden, no less. And from it will come the New Creation. Believe it.

And thank you, Simeon, for the heads-up. Yes, the thoughts of many hearts will be revealed.

> Were you there when they pierced him in the side?
> Were you there when they pierced him in the side?
> O! Sometimes it causes me to tremble! tremble!
>   tremble!
> Were you there when they pierced him in the side?
>
> Were you there when the sun refused to shine?
> Were you there when the sun refused to shine?
> O! Sometimes it causes me to tremble! tremble!
>   tremble!
> Were you there when the sun refused to shine?
>
> Were you there when they laid him in the tomb?
> Were you there when they laid him in the tomb?
> O! Sometimes it causes me to tremble! tremble!
>   tremble!
> Were you there when they laid him in the tomb?
> ("Were You There?" American Spiritual, first printed
>   in 1899.)

Ask Yourself. Share with Another.

Do I really want to change? How?

Sing it at soundtrack.seedbed.com

THURSDAY OF PASSION WEEK

The Lament of God

. . . .

I want to invite you to slow down and walk very deliberately through the following verses.

He was despised and forsaken of men, a man of sorrows and acquainted with grief; and like one from whom men hide their face He was despised, and we did not esteem Him. Surely our griefs He Himself bore, and our sorrows He carried; yet we ourselves esteemed Him stricken, smitten of God, and afflicted. But He was pierced through for our transgressions, He was crushed for our iniquities; the chastening for our well-being *fell* upon Him, and by His scourging we are healed. All of us like sheep have gone astray, each of us has turned to his own way; but the Lord has caused the iniquity of us all to fall on Him. (Isa. 53:3–6 NASB)

This is the lament of Holy Week. Watch as Isaiah 53 unfolds in Song 69.

PSALM 69

MORNING SONG   86.86 C.M.
Words by Julie Tennent based on Psalm 69

1   Save me, O God, for waters have engulfed me like
      a flood;
2   There is no foothold as I sink in miry depths, O God.

3   I've called for help, my throat is parched, and God
      cannot be found;
4   And those who hate me without cause are more than
      I can count.

   Yes, many are my enemies; their plot to kill is real,
   And I am forced to give to them what I did
      never steal.

5   You know my folly, O my God; my guilt is in plain view.
6   Let me not be a cause of shame for all who hope
      in You.

   O Lord, the Lord Almighty God, may those who seek
      Your face,
   Not be ashamed because of me; O God of
      Israel's race.

7   For I endure scorn for Your sake; my face is filled
      with shame;
8   I am a stranger to my kin, to all who share my name.

9   I am consumed with zeal, O Lord, for Your
      house fervently;
   The insults of those who curse You now fall with
      weight on me.

10   And when I weep and fast, I must endure
        scorn constantly;
11   When sackcloth is my daily garb, they all make sport
        of me.

12   Those seated at the gate mock me; they taunt with
        drunken song;
13   But to You, Lᴏʀᴅ, I pray—hear me! Your love is wide
        and long.

14   In Your salvation, answer me, and save me from
        the mire;
     Don't let me sink—deliver me! Their hatred does
        not tire.

15   Deep waters roll, the floodgates pour, the depths will
        swallow me;
     Don't let the flood engulf me or the pit close over me.

16   Lᴏʀᴅ, from the goodness of Your love, in mercy turn
        to me.
17   Don't hide Your face, for I'm distressed; come
        answer speedily.

18   Come near and rescue me, O God; redeem me from
        my foes;
19   You know I'm scorned, disgraced, and shamed; my
        enemies You know.

20   Their scorn has left me helpless and my heart is torn
        in two;
     No one gives comfort, sympathy; I have no one
        but You.

21   They gave me gall in food to eat, and vinegar to drink;
22   May their table become a trap, a snare they would
        not think.

23 Their eyes be darkened as the blind; their backs be
ever bent;
24 Pour wrath on them and let them know the anger You
have sent.

25 May their place be deserted and let none be there
to dwell;
26 For they wound those You strike, O Lord; my pain
they love to tell.

27 Charge them with crime on crime, my God; don't let
them know Your grace.
28 May they be blotted from Your book, nor live to see
Your face.

29 I am in pain and in distress; God, save and protect me;
30 And I will praise Your name in song, to God my thanks
will be.

31 And this will please the Lord far more than ox or bull
with horn;
32 The poor will see and will be glad, who seek God
night and morn.

33 The Lord hears those who cry in need; He does not
turn away.
34 Let heav'n, earth, sea, and all therein, give Him praise
every day.

35 For God will save and will rebuild the cities of Zion;
His people will possess the land of Judah, every one.

36 Their children will inherit it; all those who love
His name.
They'll dwell there, all His servants and their children,
free from shame.

Will you dare to sing now?

You've noticed by now the break with the rhythm and cadence of prior days. Why? On Maundy Thursday, the Son of God was arrested like a common criminal. There is nothing normal about today or tomorrow or any day thereafter. Our familiar pattern is gone now. There is no neatly ordered liturgy to comfort us.

FRIDAY OF PASSION WEEK

He Is Crucified

. . . .

PSALM 22

MORNING SONG, LLANGLOFFAN, or KINGSFOLD   86.86 C.M. D
Words by Julie Tennent based on Psalm 22

1 My God, my God, O why have You forsaken me,
    and why
   are You so far from saving me, while groaning words
    I cry?

2 All day, my God, to Thee I cry, yet am not heard
    by Thee;
   And in the darkness of the night, I cannot silent be.

3 But You are holy, and You are enthroned in Isr'el's
    praise.
4 Our fathers put their trust in You—deliv'rance You
    did raise.

5 When unto You they sent their cry, to them
    deliv'rance came;
   Because they put their trust in You, they were not
    put to shame.

6   But as for me, I am a worm; a man not recognized.
     I am reproached by men, and by the people am
          despised.

7   All that see me laugh me to scorn; hurl insults all
          the day;
     They nod and shake their heads at me; and
          mocking me, they say:

8   "His trust is in the LORD, that He would free him by
          his might;
     Let Him deliver him, if He in him does take delight."

9   But You brought me out of the womb, and made me
          trust in Thee;
     And even at my mother's breast You did take care
          of me.

10   From birth I was upon You cast, ev'n from the womb
          till now;
     From mother's womb You've been my God, and still
          my God art Thou.

11   Be not far off, for grief is near, and none to help
          is found;
12   Bulls compass me; bulls of Bashan encircle me
          around.

13   The lions' mouths are opened wide against me
          all the day.
     Like as a lion ravaging and roaring for his prey.

14   Like water I'm poured out, my bones all out of joint
          do part;
     Like was within my inward parts, so melted is
          my heart.

15   My strength is like a potsherd dried; my tongue
          impedes my breath;

It sticks to my mouth's roof—You lay me in the dust
    of death.

16 For dogs have compassed me about; the wicked,
    that did meet
in their assembly, circled me; they pierced my
    hands and feet.

17 I can count all my bones; and those who gloat upon
    me stare.
18 And for my garments they cast lots, my clothes
    among them share.

19 But be not far, O LORD, my strength; come quickly
    and help me.
20 From sword my soul, from pow'r of dogs, my precious
    life set free.

21 Out of the roaring lion's mouth, come rescue me
    and save;
From horns of oxen and wild beasts, You heard and
    answer gave.

22 I will declare Your name unto my brethren everywhere;
Amidst the congregation, I Your praises will declare.

23 All you who fear the LORD, praise Him; revere and
    glory tell;
All Jacob's children, honor Him—offspring of Israel.

24 For He does not despise nor scorn th' afflicted's
    suffering;
Nor hid His face from him, but heard the cry which
    he did bring.

25 Within the congregation great, my praise shall be
    of Thee;
My vows before those who fear You, shall be fulfilled
    by me.

26 The poor shall eat, and shall be filled; they also
        praise shall give
    unto the Lᴏʀᴅ, all those who seek—may your hearts
        ever live!

27 And all the ends of earth shall turn, remembering
        the Lᴏʀᴅ.
    All fam'lies of the nations shall bow down and
        praise accord.

28 For all dominion to the Lᴏʀᴅ belongs to Him alone.
    And He rules over nations all, from His almighty
        throne.

29 The rich of earth will worship; all who to the dust
        descend;
    They all shall kneel—none of them can his soul from
        death defend.

30 Descendants, then, will serve Him—all children yet
        to be.
    They will be told about the Lᴏʀᴅ, future posterity.

31 For they shall come, and shall declare His truth and
        righteousness
    unto a people yet unborn, for He has done all this..

Good Friday

Far from a day for new insight, of which I have none, I
can only approach Good Friday in the broken English of
poetry. Here's my attempt. It will remain untitled.

NIne in the morning, pardon in breath,
exhaling mercy, inhaling death.
High noon rises, justice so bright,
veiled in a shrouded eclipse of the Light.
Three o'clock now, light reappears
as breath slips away from eternity's years.
Finished He cries, creation now healed,
sowing seeds of redemption, like treasure in the field.
Into your Spirit commend outstretched hands,
revealing an unsearchable enigmatic plan.
See sun falling, despondent defeat,
sundown, friends wrenching nails from his feet.
Darkness descending, Glory entombed,
child of the Virgin, enthroned and rewombed.

We must remember, however faint and difficult it must have been, Jesus sang Song 22 from the cross. Let's kneel and join him now.

Ask Yourself. Share with Another.

Will you walk—no crawl—slowly through Song 22? Do it in honor and remembrance of Jesus. You don't have to feel it. You don't have to like it. You don't have to understand it. Just do it. It is a simple act of faithful fellowship with the Suffering One, who sang it in solidarity with all sinners for all time.

Sing it at soundtrack.seedbed.com

SATURDAY OF PASSION WEEK

He Is Buried

. . . .

Holy Saturday . . . somebody whistle.

PSALM 88

BEACH SPRING   87.87 D
Words by Julie Tennent based on Psalm 88

1 O LORD God, the God who saves me, day and night I
   cry to You.
2 Turn Your ear to hear my anguish; may my prayer
   come before You.

3 For my soul is full of trouble, and my life draws near
   the grave;
4 I'm like those who lose all strength and sink to pits
   where none can save.

5 I am counted with the dying, like the dead
   already there;
   Not remembered, even by You; fully cut off from
   Your care.

6 You have put me in the depths, and in the lowest pit
   I'm cast;
7 Your wrath lies like weight upon me, with Your waves,
   I'm drowned at last.

170

   ♨   You have taken close friends from me, made me be
        abhorred by them;
   I am trapped, cannot escape and with much grief my
        eyes are dim.

9   Yet I daily call to You, Lᴏʀᴅ; I spread out my hands
        to You;
10 Do You show the dead your wonders? Do the dead
        rise and praise You?

11 Is Your love declared in death, or in destruction, is
        faith found?
12 Are Your wonders known in darkness, or Your praise
        where there's no sound?

13 Still I cry to You for help, Lᴏʀᴅ; in the morning my
        prayers rise;
14 Why, O Lᴏʀᴅ, do You reject me, hide Your face from
        my worn eyes?

15 From my youth, I've been afflicted, close to death and
        in despair;
16 And Your wrath has swept around me, terrors kept me
        from Your care.

17 All day long those fears surround me, and engulf me
        without end;
18 You take friends and loved ones from me; darkness is
        my closest friend.

Holy Saturday

It's Saturday.
Somebody whistle.
Sow a song in the field of the sky,
cracking the seal of the stone's cold silence,

Somebody please, whistle,
like an old man walking to his own funeral
watching children play tag in the graveyard;
tombstone for home base.
It's Saturday.
Somebody whistle.

Be still and rest.

Sing it at soundtrack.seedbed.com

EASTER SUNDAY

He Is Risen!

Declare: He is risen from the dead! He is risen indeed!

PSALM 98

AZMON, ST. ANNE, or RICHMOND   86.86 C.M.
Words by Timothy Tennent based on Psalm 98

1   O sing to God a joyful song,
     For He has done great things;
     His right hand and His holy arm
     great saving pow'r do bring.

2   The LORD's salvation is made known,
     The nations see it well;
3   He has recalled His covenant,
     His love to Israel.

     The ends of all the earth have seen
     Him break the pow'r of wrong;
4   O shout for joy, you nations all,
     Burst into joyful song!

5   Sing praises with the harp and horn,
     May voices reach the sky;

6　O shout for joy before the Lord,
　　The King who reigns on high!

7　Let oceans roar and all therein,
　　All peoples of the earth;
8　Let rivers clap their joyful hands,
　　And mountains sing His worth.

9　For God the Lord is coming soon
　　to judge the world He made;
　　He'll judge the world with equity,
　　With righteousness displayed.

Stand Amazed

At the crack of dawn on Sunday, the women came to the tomb carrying the burial spices they had prepared. They found the entrance stone rolled back from the tomb, so they walked in. But once inside, they couldn't find the body of the Master Jesus.

They were puzzled, wondering what to make of this. Then, out of nowhere it seemed, two men, light cascading over them, stood there. The women were awestruck and bowed down in worship. The men said, "Why are you looking for the Living One in a cemetery? He is not here, but raised up. Remember how he told you when you were still back in Galilee that he had to be handed over to sinners, be killed on a cross, and in three days rise up?" Then they remembered Jesus' words.

They left the tomb and broke the news of all this to the Eleven and the rest. Mary Magdalene, Joanna, Mary the mother of James, and the other women with them kept telling these things to the apostles, but the apostles didn't believe a word of it, they thought they were making it all up.

But Peter jumped to his feet and ran to the tomb. He stooped to look in and saw a few grave clothes, that's all. He walked away puzzled, shaking his head. (Luke 24:1–12 THE MESSAGE)

Behold the Risen Lord

Having beheld the resurrection of Christ, let us worship the holy Lord Jesus, the only Sinless One. We venerate Your cross, O Christ, and we praise and glorify Your holy resurrection. You are our God. We know no other than You, and we call upon Your name. Come, all faithful, let us venerate Christ's holy resurrection. For behold, through the cross joy has come to all the world. Blessing the Lord always, let us praise his resurrection. For enduring the cross for us, he destroyed death by death.[9]

—John Chrysostom

Celebrate

"Christ the Lord is risen today,"
Sons of men and angels say!
Raise your joys and triumphs high,
sing ye heavens, and earth reply.

Love's redeeming work is done
Fought the fight, the battle won:
Lo! Our Sun's eclipse is o'er,
lo! He sets in blood no more.

Vain the stone, the watch, the seal;
Christ has burst the gates of hell!
Death in vain forbids him rise:
Christ hath opened paradise!

Lives again our glorious King,
where, O death, is now thy sting?
Dying once, he all doth save,
where thy victory, O grave?

Soar we now where Christ has led,
following our exalted Head,
made like him, like him we rise;
ours the cross, the grave, the skies!

King of glory, soul of bliss,
everlasting life is this;
Thee to know, thy power to prove,
thus to sing, and thus to love!

—Charles Wesley
"Christ the Lord Is Risen Today"

Sing it at soundtrack.seedbed.com

APPENDIX

WE'RE NOT SUPPOSED TO SING THOSE PSALMS, ARE WE?
APPROACHING THE IMPRECATORY PSALMS

. . . .

By Julie Tennent

One of the most frequently asked questions about singing the whole Psalter—all of the Psalms with all of the verses—is this: What about the imprecatory psalms, those psalms that call down curses on one's enemies? How do we sing them as Christians? Didn't Jesus command us to love our enemies and pray for those who persecute us? Didn't Jesus model this on the cross when he prayed, "Father, forgive them, for they know not what they do?" (Luke 23:34 ESV). Doesn't Paul command us in Romans 12:14 to bless our enemies and not curse them? If we are truly New Testament Christians, how do these psalms continue to have a place in our prayer life, or our worship life?

There are four lenses for approaching these psalms that may be helpful, but first, a few basic observations are in order. Although there are several psalms that have been categorized officially as "imprecatory psalms," there are many more psalms that contain verses of imprecation scattered throughout. The difficulty is much wider and deeper than simply relegating certain psalms as inappropriate for Christian worship, as has sometimes been suggested. In fact, "enemies" are acknowledged in the Psalms quite frequently, and the psalmist seems to feel quite comfortable letting God know what he thinks should be done about them. It is still true today that following Christ will not be kindly regarded by those in the world, and that enemies of both body and soul are just as rampant in the world as they ever were. The question is not so much about the presence of enemies as about our response to them.

To pray or sing these verses of the Psalms as a congregation will take, most assuredly, some wise guidance and counsel from the leader of worship or the pastor; and to pray them as part of private or family worship will also require prayerful submission to the Holy Spirit in our hearts. But deciding to omit these verses takes us down a much more dangerous path, for Jesus said that he did not come to abolish the law or the prophets, but to fulfill them. We cannot decide that part of God's Word is inappropriate for us, when Christ provides the lens through which all of the Old Testament is illuminated and understood. Better far to wrestle with these verses, to pray for the Lord's understanding of why they are in Holy Scripture, and to seek the understanding and deepening of faith that they will bring to us if we are willing to seek his wisdom about them. Let us consider, then, four lenses that provide a starting point for approaching these turbulent psalms.

Lens 1: Spiritual Warfare

The first lens is found in Ephesians 6:12, "For our struggle is not against flesh and blood, but against the rulers, against the authorities, against the powers of this dark world and against the spiritual forces of evil in the heavenly realms." This first lens for the imprecatory psalms is perhaps the easiest to understand. We acknowledge, with Paul, that behind all of the flesh-and-blood agents of evil and wickedness in this world, lie powers of darkness, spiritual forces, and Satan. When we consider the evil spiritual power that is at work in this world, seeking to steal, kill, and destroy (see John 10:10) everything that is good and right and holy, we can cry out with the psalmist for the Lord to put an end to these principalities of wickedness and to break their hold on the lives of people in this world.

The imprecations of the Psalms can thus be directed to the spiritual forces that lie behind all of the evil that we encounter—the spiritual powers that attempt to enslave us with addictions or haunt us with unbelief. The ravages of depression in the lives of those you love, the tyranny of poverty and injustice willfully imposed by wealthy dictators upon the poor, the horrors of rape and torture enacted upon innocent victims, the bondages of all kinds which entrap and destroy healthy lives and families—all of these enemies are the tangible outworkings of principalities and powers that we can fervently denounce along with the psalmist. Evil has many expressions, but there is no doubt that behind those tangible agents is the evil one who is at work in this world, and it is right to pray for his demise with all of the robust imprecations that the Psalms can muster.

Lens 2: Vengeance Transferred

The second lens arises from the Lord's declaration in Deuteronomy 32:35, quoted by Paul in Romans 12:19, "'It is mine to avenge; I will repay,' says the Lord." As those created in the image of God, we are hardwired for justice. We have an inner sense of right and wrong implanted in our conscience, and when wrong is done, we feel the need for it to be set right, for righteousness to be vindicated and for evil to be punished. We want the real flesh-and-blood perpetrators of evil to be punished, and the Lord has provided the avenues of government for just that purpose. However, there are times when wrong goes unpunished, when wickedness flourishes unrestrained, or when human systems of justice fail. We want to take matters into our own hands, striking back with the due retribution that we desire to inflict upon those who have wronged us. But our desire for vengeance and vindication must be transferred into God's hands, for he alone can dispense justice with true righteousness. When the psalmist calls down curses, this is precisely what he is doing. He is asking the Lord to take vengeance rather than taking it himself; he is pouring all of the anguish of reprisal into a prayer rather than into actions of his own.

When one has experienced unspeakable horror, seen family members raped and slaughtered, or been the victim of unmitigated violence, there must be a channel for the anguish and anger to pour out. If there is not, the rage will burst forth into reciprocal violence, and the escalation of evil will continue. But if anger and anguish and retribution can be expressed to God in all of their rawness, uncensored and unrestrained, then they can be released and left in the hands of the one who has also suffered and who we can trust to bring proper vindication. These psalms are, after all, prayers—not the actions themselves. In fact, the prayers offer an alternative action, providing the necessary and healthy channel for anger to be vented without erupting into violence. By taking this action, anger can be transferred into the hands of God who has promised to bring about his holy judgment with perfect equity. It is through this sometimes dark channel of expression and transference that we can emerge into the light of forgiveness and wholeness, and find the power of the Holy Spirit to walk in newness of life.

Lens 3: The Curse Absorbed

"Christ redeemed us from the curse of the law by becoming a curse for us, for it is written: 'Cursed is everyone who is hung on a pole'" (Gal. 3:13). This verse from Galatians provides the third lens for understanding the imprecatory psalms. Just as the second lens enables us to transfer our anger and need for vengeance into the Lord's hands, this lens reminds us of the terrifying reality that all of the curses that belong upon the wicked are transferred onto Christ. As we encounter the vivid descriptions of curses that are called forth in the Psalms, we are suddenly caught off guard by the stark reality that even these terrible curses (and so much more than we could ever fathom) have been laid upon Christ in the crucifixion. God hears every curse that we voice, accepts every cry for vengeance that we sob, and holds every wrong that we suffer in his cup, which Christ absorbs upon the cross. All the punishment that the wicked deserve falls upon Christ. All the curses which the fall brought into this world come upon Christ. Every imprecation that is directed to an enemy (whether spiritual or physical) is carried by Christ.

This is transference in reverse. We transfer our anger and vengeance into God's hands, and Christ takes upon himself all the wrath that we deserve (along with all that our enemies deserve). He becomes the curse. He carries our sorrows. He suffers on our behalf. He absorbs the weight of all of the wickedness, all of the evil, all of the demonic onslaught, all of the imprecations, and all of the righteous wrath due for sin—it is all absorbed and extinguished as he cries, "It is finished." When we voice these imprecations, we see more vividly the depth of the love of Christ, who became a curse for us.

Lens 4: The Final End

The fourth lens is that of eschatology—the unfolding of final things. Revelation 11:15: "The kingdom of the world has become the kingdom of our Lord and of his Messiah, and he will reign for ever and ever." Though Christ has taken the curse for all who trust in him, the judgment of God will still come upon all those who do not take refuge in him. Many of the imprecations in the Psalms carry an element of finality to them; they evoke bold images of total and permanent destruction. These curses seem very frightening unless we remember that our greatest hope lies in God setting all things right in his New Creation. The ultimate goal toward which all of creation is heading is the joyous rule and reign of God, where evil is banished forever, never to rise again.

The judgment of God upon the forces of wickedness is not something to be feared—it is our greatest hope and comfort. Indeed, the judgment of God against the wicked is the way in which God demonstrates his love and mercy for the world. For example, Psalm 137:8–9 has often troubled Christians, but we must see the larger eschatological vision. When the infant children of evil Babylon (who represent Babylon's ability to regenerate and carry on her wickedness) are utterly destroyed (as God himself predicted in Isaiah 13), it is God's fulfillment of his long-awaited promise that there will be a time when sin and evil, darkness and death, wickedness and depravity, will all be ended, never to rise again. God is the one who will do this.

> "Fallen! Fallen is Babylon the Great! . . . With such violence the great city of Babylon will be thrown down, never to be found again. . . . Hallelujah! Salvation and glory and power belong to our God, for true and just are his judgments. He has condemned the great prostitute who corrupted the

earth by her adulteries. He has avenged on her the blood of his servants. . . . Hallelujah! For our Lord God Almighty reigns. Let us rejoice and be glad and give him glory!" (Rev. 18:2, 21; 19:1–2, 6–7).

This is the great hope of Christians. Someday, there will be a final end to all evil, and it will never rear its ugly head again. Someday, there will be a final end to all suffering, and we will live in the New Creation with no tears, no sorrow, no pain, and no death. But this can only come about if the Lord God puts an end to wickedness once and for all, a victory that was secured in the cross of Christ, but awaits consummation at the final judgment. The imprecations, which cry out for this final destruction, for this definitive end to evil, are pointers to that great hope. They should fill us with longing for that day, and with great hope in the present that God's victory is secure, and that someday the enemy of our souls will haunt us no more. These psalms are pointers, reminders, and beacons of hope in our God who has triumphed over sin and death, and will bring both to a final end.

NOTES

1. Dietrich Bonhoeffer, *Psalms: The Prayer Book of the Bible* (Minneapolis, MN: Augsburg Publishing House, 1970), 26.
2. John Calvin, *Calvin's Commentaries: The First Epistle of Paul the Apostle to the Corinthians*, trans. John W. Fraser, eds. David W. Torrance and Thomas F. Torrance (Grand Rapids, MI: William B. Eerdmans Publishing Company, 1960), 210.
3. Ambrose was Archbishop of Milan and wrote this in his *Commentary on the Psalms* around AD 385, quoted in Phil Moore, *Straight to the Heart of Psalms: 60 Bite-Sized Insights* (Grand Rapids, MI: Monarch Books, 2013), 142.
4. Nicetas of Remesiana (circa 410).
5. John Wesley, *The Works of the Reverend John Wesley* (New York: B. Waugh and T. Mason, 1835), 82.
6. Now, this reflection is not a veiled knock on antidepressants, which are very helpful in many cases. Sometimes people's inner chemistry can be so confounded that it takes a chemical intervention to get them to a stable enough place where they can lament. As a wise pastor once told me, medication will not solve your problems, but it can help you fight your battles.
7. Charles H. Spurgeon, *The Treasury of David: Classic Reflections on the Wisdom of the Psalms* (Peabody, MA: Hendrickson Publishers, 1990), 464.
8. Ibid.
9. Seraphim Nassar, *Divine Prayers and Services of the Catholic Orthodox Church of Christ,* 3rd ed. (Englewood, NJ: Antiochian Orthodox Christian Archdiocese of North America, 1979), 935–36.